50 GREAT MOMENTS IN PITTSBURGH SPORTS

From the Flying Dutchman to Sid the Kid

David Shribman
and Richard "Pete" Peterson

GV584.5.P57 S57 2012
Shribman, David M.
50 great moments in
Pittsburgh sports : from the
Flying Dutchman to Sid the
Kid
Chicago : Triumph Books,

TRIUMPH
BOOKS

Library of Congress Cataloging-in-Publication Data
Shribman, David M.
  50 great moments in Pittsburgh sports : from the Flying Dutchman to Sid the Kid / David Shribman and Richard 'Pete' Peterson.
    p. cm.
  Includes bibliographical references and index.
  ISBN 978-1-60078-762-1 (alk. paper)
  1. Sports—Pennsylvania—Pittsburgh—History. 2. Athletes—Pennsylvania—Pittsburgh—History. I. Peterson, Richard F. II. Title. III. Title: Fifty great moments in Pittsburgh sports.
  GV584.5.P57S57 2012
  796.09748'86—dc23
                    2012020211

This book is available in quantity at special discounts for your group or organization. For further information, contact:
  Triumph Books LLC
  814 N. Franklin Street
  Chicago, Illinois 60610
  (312) 337-0747
  Fax (312) 280-5470

Printed in the United States of America
ISBN 978-1-60078-762-1

All photographs courtesy of the *Pittsburgh Post-Gazette*, except where otherwise indicated

Pittsburgh Post-Gazette
John Robinson Block, Co-publisher and Editor-in-Chief
David M. Shribman, Executive Editor and Vice-President
Susan L. Smith, Managing Editor
Mary Leonard, Deputy Managing Editor

RESEARCH
Angelika Kane
Taryn Luna

ADMINISTRATIVE COORDINATOR
Allison Alexander, Marketing Manager

CONTENTS

PREFACE

By David M. Shribman
Executive Editor, *Pittsburgh Post-Gazette*

Moments, moments. The history of sports is but a collection of moments.

First there are national moments. The time Carlton Fisk, with his hands, his legs, and all the power of his heart, virtually willed a hard-hit ball over the fence in the sixth game of the 1975 World Series at Fenway Park. The time Johnny Unitas drove the Baltimore Colts down the field in an overtime NFL championship game in 1958 that ended when Alan Ameche scored from the 1-yard line and that began pro football's reign as a great American sport. The time a scraggly group of Americans pulled off a miracle on ice and beat the Soviets in a Cold War confrontation on American territory, in an arena at Lake Placid.

Then there are our personal moments, and we can all list our own. For Pete Peterson, it was playing catch in a South Side alley with his father and going out to Oakland and its most alluring attraction, the old ballyard on Forbes Avenue. For me, it was being taken by my father and grandfather to my first Red Sox game, a no-hitter as it turned out, performed by the graceful Earl Wilson on a beautiful June night four months before the missiles would be discovered in Cuba. And it was taking my wife and daughter, clad in black and gold, to watch Troy Polamalu make the interception that sent our beloved Steelers to the Super Bowl in 2008.

And finally there are our town's memories: those magic evenings swinging Terrible Towels after Super Bowl victories. The stories about Duquesne basketball teams of yore. The cries of *chicken on the hill* and *here we go!* and *let's go Pitt!*, the strains of "We Are Family" and "Renegade." And of perhaps the worst 24 hours in Pittsburgh sports, when Pitt was denied an Orange Bowl appearance and the Steelers were denied a victory over the Raiders with two last-20-second pass receptions in the very same chilly end zone in December 2009.

Sporting events are not the most important things we do. We are born, are educated, get married, have kids, and then die. All those things are more important than any game. Our country elects presidents, goes to war, suffers from economic downturns, enjoys boom periods, endures crises. No comparison. But maybe because the games we watch are so less important—maybe because they are diversions from the important things—that we keep them with us, year after year, through boom and bust, war and peace, personal triumphs, family tragedies. They are our companions.

No one alive in Pittsburgh on December 23, 1972 (and many thousands born long after), walks this Earth without a memory of what Franco Harris did against a stunned Oakland Raiders team at Three Rivers Stadium. We go through our days remembering where we were when Forbes Field closed, when Mario Lemieux retired, when Roberto Clemente died. We shared the joy of Carnegie Tech when it beat Notre Dame and of Santonio Holmes when his feet caught the corner of a Super Bowl end zone, and we shared the heartbreak of Billy Conn in the 13th round or of the Penguins in Game 6 of the 2008 Stanley Cup Final.

Here in Pittsburgh we have had our moments, many scores of them, more than our share. Carnegie Tech was once a great football power, and so once long ago was Duquesne, and in more recent years so was Pitt. College basketball has thrived here, both the male and female variety, the Civic Arena for some fleeting moments seeming like our local Palestra, and we have had a few strong cups of coffee with pro basketball. Hockey is a language and religion all its own, spoken and practiced here. And if you are younger than 19 years old you will have to take my word for this, but baseball has thrived in our neighborhood for more than a century, and we have the pennants to prove it.

So when Pete Peterson, professor and professed sports nut, and I came up with the idea of collecting the greatest sports stories in *Post-Gazette* history, we had a challenge on our hands. He grew up here but didn't live here anymore, and I grew up elsewhere but live here now. Together we covered a lot of territory, but not all. We enlisted the help of the late Phil Musick, longtime sportsman and a journalist possessed of a great memory, to fill in some of the gaps, and then the two of us, Pete and I, put together a couple of draft lists—just like the pros do, though we had the advantage of knowing how things turned out. And with the indispensable help of Angelika Kane and Taryn Luna, two *Post-Gazette* staff members who helped us assemble this book, we started reading the original stories about the events for which we had only heard stories.

You won't find everything in here. The second Pens' Stanley Cup, for example, is missing, and not because we didn't have great respect for Larry

Murphy and Tom Barrasso, Bob Errey and Bryan Trottier. A labor dispute kept the *Post-Gazette* from publishing, so your best bet is to go to YouTube and hear Mike Lange cry, "Lord Stanley, Lord Stanley, get me the brandy." Many of your favorites probably have been omitted as well. We have a file of things that didn't make it, including a 1921 story about a Pirates win streak over the Phillies that captures both the tone of the time and the sportswriting of the time: "It was the fourth consecutive success for the Buccos and the third straight victory over the Quakers, the first game of the set having been postponed by rain." No one writes stories like that anymore, but then again the Bucs don't beat the Phils three in a row anymore either.

You will find a lot of your memories between these covers, and a lot of stories that will re-create your parents' memories. We have title fights and twin bowl victories performed by Pitt and Duquesne (Rose and Orange, 1937). We have Calder Cups and Arnold Palmer at the Masters. We have Beaver Falls defeating Aliquippa in a WPIAL basketball championship and a Triangles title, Don Hennon's 45 points in a double-overtime game against Duke, a Pitt Olympic gold medal, and Tony Dorsett breaking an all-time rushing record—and much, much more.

But in unearthing all of these stories—in finding some of the truly golden needles hiding in the *Post-Gazette*'s haystack, itself nearly two and a quarter centuries in the making—Pete and I made a discovery richer than any one of the hundred we assembled in this volume. We found that sports, which we thought was the ultimate shared experience, was above all a personal experience. It was the games we saw, the stories we had only heard about, the moments we remembered, that mattered. There was, of course, the roar of the crowd in almost every one of these pages you are about to turn. But it is our conviction that the strongest sound you will hear is the murmur of your own heart and the stirrings of your own spirit. Sport does that to us, and for us.

First Pirates World Series Championship

1909

In 1909 the Pittsburgh Pirates finished with a record-setting 110 wins and dethroned the powerful Chicago Cubs, winners of the last three National League pennants. After losing the 1903 World Series, the first in major league history, the Pirates finally had a chance to redeem themselves in the 1909 World Series. Led by Honus Wagner, the Pirates split the first six games against Ty Cobb's powerful Detroit Tigers. In the seventh and deciding game, played in Detroit, player-manager Fred Clarke decided to pitch rookie Babe Adams. With Adams pitching a shutout and Wagner clinching the victory with a clutch triple, the Pirates routed the Tigers 8–0 and claimed the first major sports championship in Pittsburgh's modern sports history—in the first year the team played its games at the fabled Forbes Field.

PIRATES ARE WORLD CHAMPIONS, 8 TO 0; "BABE" ADAMS HERO OF PITTSBURGH FANDOM

Tigers Annihilated by Invincible Band Under the Picaroon Banner

Fred Clarke's Marauders Carry Off Hide of Jungle King in Final Invasion of His Lair

Wild Bill Donovan Lives Up to His Name

October 17, 1909
By Edward F. Balinger
The Pittsburgh Gazette Times

DETROIT—October 15—High over a slain Tiger tonight, the Pirate pennant of victory heralds that Pittsburgh has won the most stubbornly contested series of games for the world's baseball championship ever played.

"Babe" Adams, the wonder Fred Clarke brought from the Blue Grass realm, again took the measure of Hughie Jennings' pride, and its colors trailed in the dust of defeat by a score of 8 to 0.

From the moment the first of Clarke's warriors stepped to the plate the slaughter began.

There was no let-up.

Teams Fought for Every Point

The National League players mean to keep the championship, and fought every inch of the way until the last man was out in the ninth. Even after the lead was so great that victory was practically assured, the Pittsburghers kept up the killing pace.

Nothing daunted them; they were determined on victory in this last chance, and took it, giving nothing in return.

"Wild Bill" Donovan tackled the Pirates first. They ate him up. Bill was entirely to their liking, and after the dejected Tiger leader saw there was no chance with his fair-weather pitcher, Mullin was again called into the game, but the strain of the three games of the series he had already pitched was too severe and he was as easy for the eagle-eyed batters from the "Smoky City" as Donovan had been.

Pirates in Splendid Form

The Pirates were in splendid form, and completely outclassed the Tiger aggregation at every stage of the game. The one regrettable feature was that Bobby Byrne met with an injury, which put him out of the game and will cripple him for some time. It happened in the first inning, when the little infielder was sliding for third. He collided with Moriarty and sprained an ankle.

The accident made a shift in the lineup necessary. "Bill" Abstein, believing he could not regain his real form, had been slated for the bench, and "Ham" Hyatt warmed up at first base to try his hand at the position he once occupied in the minors of the Far West. This plan was abandoned when Byrne went down and out with a severely sprained ankle.

"Tommy" Leach was transferred to third base, Hyatt played center, and Abstein resumed his old stand at the initial pillow. With the team thus patched up, the Pirates played the same classy ball that marked their work in the opening game at Pittsburgh.

After the conclusion of the struggle, Detroit took on the aspect of a town inhabited solely by Pittsburghers. Tiger rooters took in their horns and whistles and wandered about the streets, sadly listening to the merry screams of the proud fans from Pennsylvania, and trying to realize what had hit them.

Rooters Spur Players On

Every rooter who ever lived in Allegheny County appeared to have closed the house and brought his family out to join in the celebration. These added to the thousand or thereabouts of Smoketown's faithful, who came here to see the great dispute settled, were sufficient to make Rome howl, and they did that very thing with all the energy within them. Pandemonium reigned in Detroit tonight, and that is enough said.

The largest delegation from Pittsburgh today was fortunate enough to secure seats in the grandstand just back of home plate, and it was the cheering of this bunch that could be at times heard above the din of the throng that filled Bennett Park. The Pittsburghers were armed to the teeth with tin pans, foghorns, rattlers, megaphones, and bells.

Fight Way Through Crowds

When in the second inning, the Pirates started putting runs across the plate, the "Jungle" residents closed up their clams, leaving their rival rooters to continue alone.

After the fray, the Smoketown faction made a rush for Hotel Ponchartrain, where the Pirates have been quartered. Five thousand persons were lined around the 12-story hostelry in less than no time, all eager for a parting glimpse of the real champions.

When the taxicabs drew up before the entrance, the ball players found it necessary to fairly fight their way across the flagstones. Everybody was making a grab for the heroes, and they were kept busy shaking hands. Hans Wagner, Tommy Leach, Fred Clarke, and George Gibson were literally carried into the building, and Charlie Adams was fairly picked to pieces.

The mob got hold of "Babe" after he entered the corridor, and he was instantly surrounded. They hugged him, slapped him on the back, wrung his hands and howled about him like a band of Indians.

Three Cheers; No Tiger

Adams finally managed to get away and dart into one of the elevators, but they yanked him bodily out, and gave three cheers for him that fairly shook the marble walls. At last the big youth succeeded in squeezing into an elevator, the operator slammed the door and "Babe" made the escape of his life.

Every member of the club passed through some similar ordeal and the relic hunters twisted away sections of their clothing to be cherished as souvenirs. President Barney Dreyfuss was held up in front of the hotel office for more than an hour and his hands heartily shaken by hundreds of leading citizens and men well known in baseball circles.

Secretary William H. Locke was also the central figure for a similar reception. Manager Fred Clarke escaped to his rooms as quickly as he could, but he was halted many times and widely congratulated by admiring fans.

Play Well All Around

Pittsburgh's wonderful work at bat, on the bases, and in the field made the Tigers stand aghast. They played the sort of ball that nobody can beat. Deacon Phillippe and Babe Adams were both warming up before the fun began and each seemed to be in perfect condition, but Clarke finally selected the youngster, who had already won two of the three games, and he made good once more.

George Chip KOs Fred Klaus for Middleweight Title

1913

The Pirates may have given the city its first professional championship, but its boxers gave Pittsburgh its first claim to being the city of champions. It's unusual when a title fight features boxers from the same area, but that's what happened when New Castle's George Chip challenged Pittsburgh native and middleweight champion, Fred Klaus, for the title. Chip was a heavy underdog for the match and lightly regarded by Klaus, but it only took one punch for Chip to overcome the odds and Klaus' taunting to become the middleweight champion. Chip and Klaus met three months later, and the underdog Chip knocked out Klaus again to defend his title. Despite the defeat, Pittsburgh's Klaus had a distinguished career and was eventually enshrined in the Boxing Hall of Fame.

FRANK KLAUS IS STOPPED BY GEORGE CHIP

Miner Renders Middleweight Champion Incapable to Continue With Punch to Jaw

Comes in Sixth Round

October 12, 1913
By Richard Guy
The Pittsburgh Gazette Times

Frank Klaus, recognized as the champion middleweight fighter of the world, ran into a right hook to the jaw in the sixth round delivered by George Chip, the Madison miner, last night at Old City Hall, and was rendered incapable of continuing. His head came in contact with the hard floor of the ring, and he was dazed and unfit to fight any more and the referee waved Chip to his corner.

Klaus has been fighting over eight years, and in that time he has met all the tough boys of the middleweight division, sometimes entering the heavy-weight plane and he was never knocked off his feet or never compelled to listen to the tolling off of seconds by a referee.

But last night it was different. He entered the ring for the exhibition with the spirit of a man going out for a frolic.

He did not consider Chip a man worthy of his mettle and that he had done no training for the bout was apparent by the extra weight around his belt and his shortage of wind when they worked fast.

There never was a time during the first five rounds that Chip had a chance and there were many times when Klaus appeared to be holding back his punches, which occasioned comment around the ring. "He can't keep the pig if he eats it," was a suggestive comment by a former boxer, which means that Klaus was looking for a future bout with the same opponent.

But Chip was doing his best: there never was a time when he let down in his work and his courage was unlimited, although a few times he covered to escape punches and at this time Klaus held back and allowed him to take a better position.

Chip is a fighter who was never rated as a champion or a championship contender, but he was recognized as a man who possesses a terrible wallop and game to the core. He takes fighting seriously, while Klaus, the sturdy man who could allow adversaries to hit him from swings to the jaw and never flinch, the owner of a veritable iron jaw, takes his average bout as matter of no concern. But it proved to be his undoing, and that night when Chip sneaked in that hook to the jaw and the champion went down on the flat of his back, the crowd could hardly believe it. His friends were astonished as were those who were shouting for Chip.

The victor came in for a great reception. Klaus climbed through the rope and on his way to the dressing room remarked: "It was my own fault. I held him too cheap. Being knocked down is a sensation new to me. I did not try for a knockout at any stage, but Chip had one real chance and he took it."

"One good chance" just about describes the fight. For five rounds Klaus fought as though he was working out in a gymnasium. Chip was worked hard all the time, but when he led, Klaus warded off his punches, and when he felt like it he sent his right or left to the body, but there was not the viciousness to these punches that characterized his former fights. He paid more attention to boxing and during the intermission between the round he joked and chatted with his manager George Engel, and Billy Reynolds, a Philadelphia friend.

The fight up to this time could not be considered a good exhibition, for seldom did Klaus cut loose with any real work and Chip seemed so easy for him to handle. But suddenly, like the proverbial lightning from a clear sky, out went that punch and Klaus went down. He got up, but he was dazed and the bout was stopped. Less than 10 seconds remained to the end of the round.

Hooks Evans won from Harry Greb in six rounds and Jimmy McCoy and Johnny Ray boxed a draw. Young Tooley had a lead on Johnny Cook.

3

Pitt Defeats Georgia Tech and Claims Third National Championship

1918

After an eight-year stint with the Carlisle Indians and the great Jim Thorpe, the legendary Glenn "Pop" Warner signed on to coach the Pitt Panthers beginning with the 1915 season. The Panthers went undefeated in 1915 and 1916 and were declared national champions. Pitt remained undefeated in 1917, but John Heisman's Georgia Tech team claimed the national championship. Both Pitt and Georgia Tech were undefeated in 1918 when they met at Forbes Field. In a season shortened by war and an influenza epidemic, the powerful Georgia Tech team had averaged 84 points per game and had scored 128 points against North Carolina State. But with All-American freshman Tom Davies leading the way, Pitt shut out Georgia Tech and claimed its third national championship under Pop Warner.

PITT MASTERS GEORGIA TECH; SCORE 32-0

Southern Champions Defeated by Warner's Men at Forbes Field

Thirty Thousand People See Golden Tornado Dimmed by Ferocious Panther in Which Famous Jump Shift Fails Utterly to Baffle Local Gridiron Stars.

Visitors Are Not Equipped With Ground-Gaining Plays

November 24, 1918

By Richard Guy

The Pittsburgh Gazette Times

The University of Pittsburgh once more arose to the height of its power in football and smote a killing blow to a much-heralded adversary when it vanquished Georgia Tech representatives yesterday afternoon at Forbes Field, 32 to 0, in the presence of an estimated crowd of 30,000 people. The luster of the Golden Tornado, which swept aside all opposition south of the Mason and Dixon Line the past several years, was badly dimmed by the ferocity of the Panther. Pitt now is the undisputed collegiate champion of America, clinching the title in a game for the benefit of the United War Fund drive.

There was nothing fluky about the victory, for Pitt showed a superiority over its worthy opponent from Atlanta in a masterly fashion. So decisive was the victory, and the means whereby it was encompassed so convincing that not one iota of doubt existed in the mind of any person in the park long before the final whistle blew. Tech was out-matched in individual and collective efforts, and infinitely so in teamwork. The marked superiority of Pitt was manifested from the very start, and not once during the entire contest did the status of things change.

The famous jump shift of Tech, which could not be stopped by opponents heretofore, was negligible yesterday. There was nothing baffling in its deception to the Pitt foemen. Much was expected of the Tech team and little did it show.

The Tech team was impressive when it came on the field ahead of Pitt. The players are lithe, long-limbed, and strong, built for speed and endurance. They looked formidable and to the close observer it was not hard to discern from a physical viewpoint why they had come north with a record of victories and high scores unsurpassed in the history of Southern football. They were attired in a novel manner, too, for they wore golden jerseys and white stockings, with guards, fore and after. And they warmed up with the abandon of a field of great trotters in a classic, confidence portrayed in their faces and every move. But they were good-looking only, for subsequent events proved that they had not come to Pittsburgh equipped with ground-gaining formations and plays capable of combating such a versatile opponent as Pitt. Tech was not only whipped in a physical sense but was outwitted and outclassed.

Pitt halfback Tommy Davies was an All-American in 1918 and 1920. (*Post-Gazette* archives)

Pitt had a diversified attack, so bewildering in its nature that Tech was unable to fathom it, and of the five touchdowns scored Pitt started three of them by the medium of overhead attack, while Tech had no adequate defense to thwart them. Tech showed it is a champion in a slower class.

4

Harry Greb Decisions Gene Tunney for Light-Heavyweight Title

1923

Munhall's Harry Greb was one of the greatest fighters in boxing history. Known as "the Pittsburgh Windmill," he had the ferocity of a street fighter in the ring. In his career, he fought in nearly 300 bouts and, while suffering two TKOs, was never knocked out. He won the light-heavyweight title from Gene Tunney in 1922 and the middleweight title from Johnny Wilson the following year. He also successfully defended his middleweight title against the welterweight champion, Mickey Walker. Greb fought Tunney five times. In their first bout, Greb soundly defeated the previously undefeated light-heavyweight champion. A few months later, Tunney regained his crown from Greb in a controversial decision. After two draws, Tunney soundly defeated Greb in their fifth and final meeting. Tunney claimed that in his loss to Greb in their first meeting, he suffered the most savage beating of his career.

GREB LIGHT-HEAVY CHAMPION

Pittsburgher Wins U.S. Title in 15-Round Battle with Tunney

Ten Thousand Fistiana Followers in Madison Square Garden, New York, See Hitherto Undefeated Ex-Soldier Lose Laurels in Grueling Bout—Blood Pours from Eye, Nose, Mouth

May 24, 1922
By Harry Keck
Special Telegram to the *Gazette Times*

NEW YORK—May 23—The dope panned out properly in Madison Square Garden tonight when Harry Greb, Pittsburgh's greatest fighter, left the ring at the conclusion of a hard 15-round bout with Gene Tunney. He was the new American light-heavyweight champion, and the logical next opponent for a battle with Georges Carpentier for the championship of the world at 175 pounds.

Greb won the decision of the two judges and the referee.

There was little doubt that the officials would give the award to the man who had entered the ring the challenger, and when the announcement was made the house let loose a roar of approval.

The crowd did not come up to expectations considering that a championship was involved in the main event. The advance sale of tickets was considerably below par, and, although the fans came in large numbers in the last couple of hours the capacity of the Garden was not tested. The attendance was probably about 10,000.

Tunney put up the great fight the writer expected of him. He was not good enough to beat down the ever-rushing Pittsburgher, but he went to his defeat at least with the heart of a champion.

Tunney Hits Solidly

He stood up and fought all the time and there were several times during the contest when Greb did not have things all his own way. Tunney hit solidly to the head and body, particularly to the body with both hands. A few times he popped Greb squarely on the chin with a heavy right, but as usual such punishment merely made Greb fight back harder.

Up until tonight Tunney had never been beaten in a bout. He fought his way through the A.E.F and won the light-heavyweight championship of the Army in France. Upon his return to this country he won every bout in which he participated and won the championship from Battling Levinsky in the same ring in which he met defeat tonight.

Gibbons Easier than Gene

Greb found Tommy Gibbons a much easier man to beat than he did Tunney. Gibbons was slow and did not do one-tenth the hard fighting that Tunney put across. Gene showed his pluck after getting away with a most discouraging start. His nose bled from a punch received in the first mix-up of the fight and the crimson smeared his features.

In the sixth round his left eye was badly cut and the gore poured from it throughout the remainder of the bout. In the latter rounds he was bleeding from the eye, nose and mouth. Greb left the ring unmarked except for some puffing around the face.

The two men fought at a terrific clip until Tunney tired in the last three rounds. Harry was in great condition and fast, but he did not appear to be as speedy as he was when he defeated Tommy Gibbons here on March 13. This was due to the fact that Tunney also was fast and kept moving around with him.

Greb Follows Rushing Tactics

Greb fought his usual rushing bout, while Tunney confined most of his efforts to trying to catch him coming in and score with swings to the body. He planted a number of these and after the first four or five rounds they appeared to have their effect on Greb, but Harry's wonderful vitality came to his aid and he got back into his best stride again.

Greb weighed in at 162¼ pounds at 2 o'clock this afternoon. Tunney's weight was 174½ pounds.

Tunney was popular with the crowd. He received a tremendous ovation when he entered the ring, probably due as much to his war reputation as his ring fighting ability. Greb also was well received. Greb entered the ring the favorite and at vague odds. The wagering was abnormally light. The Greb people for the most part were unable to get down their money.

Little Cash Back of Tunney

In the lobby of the Pennsylvania Hotel, where the Pittsburgh delegation held forth, wild rumors were circulated from time to time to the effect that Tunney backers were willing to offer 1 to 2 or 1 to 2½ on their favorite, but none of the money could be corralled. The Tunney backers simply weren't on the scene. They gave Gene their moral support but feared to place their coin against the chances of Greb.

At several times during the bout the fighting was so hot that the spectators jumped and cheered. In the thirteenth round when Tunney suddenly staged a rally after winning the proceeding round, one excited spectator flipped his brand-new straw hat into the ring and it passed out on the other side.

Greb's Plans Indefinite

Tunney was a far better fighter tonight than he was when he recently appeared before a Pittsburgh crowd and knocked out John Burke. He looked better in defeat tonight than he did in victory on the former occasion. He was every bit worthy of Greb's mettle and Harry whipped a good man and a game one when he added his first title to a long string of conquests.

Greb's plans for the immediate future are indefinite. The chances are however that he will not appear in any but important bouts for at least several months.

5

Pirates World Series Victory over the Washington Senators

1925

After a 16-year absence, the Pirates returned to the World Series to face the defending world champion Washington Senators. The Senators had a star-studded roster, including future Hall-of-Famers Sam Rice, Goose Goslin, and the great Walter Johnson, but the Pirates had their own Hall-of-Famers with Max Carey, Kiki Cuyler, and Pie Traynor. When the Pirates fell behind three games to one against the Senators, they were branded cowards by the local press, but the Pirates rallied to win the next two games and set the stage for a seventh and deciding game. No team had ever overcome a 3–1 deficit to win a best-of-seven World Series, but in the fog and rain at Forbes Field, the Pirates rallied in the bottom of the eighth against Walter Johnson and went on to a 9–7 victory on a dramatic two-out, bases-loaded, two-run double by Kiki Cuyler. After the World Series, the Pirates were praised for their courage.

PIRATES WIN WORLD SERIES CHAMPIONSHIP

Greatest Series Windup In History Sets 45,000 Wild

Thrills Follow So Fast, Fans Groggy— Mighty Johnson Falls as Pirate Bats Tinkle

October 16, 1925
By Chester L. Smith
The Pittsburgh Gazette Times

Their coronation march the hoarse, exultant shouts of 45,000 persons suddenly struck stark raving mad, the Pittsburgh Pirates yesterday were crowned the baseball champions of the world, deposing the Washington Senators in a wild, exotic struggle that will be engraved on the pages of the sport's chronicle as the greatest ever played. The score was 9 to 7.

The setting so weird that it might well have been in another world—a fog-wrapped field, clouds that scowled as they seemed to brush the top of the stands, and a continuous tattoo of rain—the Pirates climaxed a gallant comeback against obstacles that seemed almost insurmountable.

Fans in Riot of Joy

As the last put-out was made, a called strike on Leon Goslin, Washington left fielder, there was enacted a riotous scene that perhaps has never been equaled in baseball as the feverish thousands in the stands and bleachers, their emotions aroused to a degree bordering on collapse, tore aside the barriers that separated them from the field and swarmed onto the diamond. Police were helpless to stem the human tidal wave that swept toward the Pittsburgh bench and the blast upon blast of cheers that continued for half an hour or more until they have reached the ears of the saddened Washington fans in the National Capital.

New Corsair heroes were acclaimed as the National League Champions strode through to triumph. There was Carson Bigbee, once a regular but of late only a substitute, whose stinging two-base hit scored the run

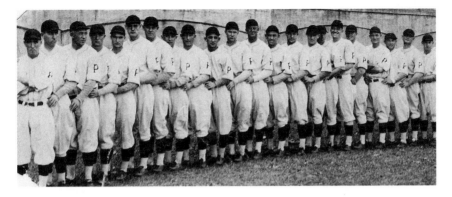

The Pittsburgh Pirates 1925 World Series championship team. (*Post-Gazette* archives)

that deadlocked the game in the eighth inning; there was Rube Oldham, pitching derelict, finally washed ashore in Pittsburgh, who hurled the ninth inning and fanned Rice and Goslin; there was Kiki Cuyler, upon whose ears must have fallen the whispers of "quitter" in previous games, who yesterday crashed the double to right that sent the winning run over the plate.

Tragedy, too, stalked on the diamond and robbed one of baseball's greatest performers and one of its most perfect gentlemen of an ambition he had pursued for 30 years.

There were few who wept for Walter Johnson in Pittsburgh yesterday, but a nation mourned as the Pirates struck one savage blow after another, until they had deluged him with 15 hits. Unfortunately, Johnson was an enemy of the Buccaneers. He had to be laid low to swing the banner of world supremacy from the Pirate masthead. So Pittsburgh, too, although joyful, may pause to pay homage to a strong-hearted fighter who remained with his team to the last.

Johnson Wanted to Stay In

Had Johnson won yesterday, he would have tied the performances of Christy Mathewson, Babe Adams, and Stanley Coveleski for the honor of pitching three victories in a single World Series. Twice he had laid a paralyzing hand on the Corsair batsmen, wining the first and fourth games by scores of 4 to 1 and 4 to 0. Yesterday with but three days of rest, be sought a third triumph.

Carefully, precisely, Johnson pitched to the Pirates, calling into play all the mastery of his command. It was his desire, spoken to Manager Bucky Harris before the game, that he be allowed to remain on the mound regardless of the outcome. And Bucky acquiesced.

There was something lacking, however, in Johnson's hurling, or perhaps there was some new spark of fire in the Pirate bats that had not been there before. At any rate, they hit him safely in every inning except the sixth; they dropped barrage after barrage of base blows into safe territory; they pounded and clubbed the best Johnson had.

To the Pirates, the battle must have been one of alternate despair and hope before the realization of their dream came in the gathering dusk of the eighth inning. Despair as their every move went wrong in the opening inning and the Senators gained what then appeared to be an overwhelming lead of four runs. Hope as they rallied in the third to come within a single tally of knotting the count. Despair again as the Nats countered in the fourth with two more tallies, increasing their lead to three. Encouragement for their refusal to admit defeat when one run brought them to even terms with their opponents for the first time. A sickening leap ahead by the Senators in the first of the eighth, and finally, the fiery, all-consuming blast that produced a trio of tallies and the championship.

Four Pirate Pitchers Used

Four Pittsburgh pitchers were on the mound during the nine innings: Victor Aldridge, John Dewey Morrison, Ray Kremer, and Rube Oldham were effective. The Senators were able to get but seven hits from the quartet, but these were bunched and were abetted by faulty pitching and two errors by Moore and Cuyler. The Pirates faced disaster at the very outset when Aldridge, returned to pitch with two days of rest, cracked wide open.

Rice, whose two hits yesterday gave him 12 and a tie with Buck Herzog for the World Series record, opened the game with a single to center. Stanley Harris flied to Barnhart, but on a wild pitch Rice went to second. Goslin then walked and he went to second and Rice went to third when Aldridge again pitched wild. A base on balls to Joe Harris filled the bases and when Judge also walked, Rice was forced in with the initial run. Bluege followed with a crackling single to left, Goslin scoring.

Morrison took Aldridge's place on the hill. On Roger Peckinpaugh's infield tap, the batter was interfered with by catcher Earl Smith and he was sent to first, while Joe Harris tallied. Moore muffed Ruel's grounder long enough to allow Judge to go home and the batter took first safely. Morrison struck out Johnson and propelled Rice, who was batting for the second time in the inning, to fly deep in left field to Barnhart.

Carey's double—his first of four safe hits—was the lone Pirate blow struck against Johnson in the first. The pitcher had tossed our Moore before Carey appeared and he followed by fanning Cuyler and Barnhart.

Two singles by Wright and McInnis signaled the approaching downfall of Johnson in the Pittsburgh half of the second, but Smith hit into a double play. Stanley Harris taking the bounder, tagging out McInnis as the latter sped down the base path, and tossing to Judge to get the batter.

Then Pirates Start

Then there came the first of the Pirates' two more substantial slugging orgies. Morrison combed Johnson for a lusty single to center and completed the circuit when Moore lined a double against the screen in left field. Carey shot Moore across the plate with a howling single over Stanley Harris' head, moved to second on Cuyler's infield tap on which Cuyler was exterminated by Bluege, and scored when Barnhart launched a one-baser to right. Traynor forced Barnhart at second, Bluege to Manager Harris, and Wright brought the Pirates to within one run of their rivals.

The Senators immediately added two to their total. Johnson had skied to Carey when Rice poked a hit to right field for one base. Manager Harris was called out on strikes, but when Goslin hit a fast pitch to third, the Goose sprinted to second on the throw to try and nip Rice. Both tallied when Joe Harries drove a spanking double to center field. The inning ended when Judge flied to Cuyler.

With none out in the fifth, the Buccos regained a portion of the gloss they had lost on successive doubles by Carey and Cuyler. Max pulled his hit into right and Kiki brought the captain home with an equally hard hit to left. Meanwhile Ray Kremer had taken up the pitching burden for the Pirates, Grantham having batted for Morrison in the unproductive half of the fourth. For three innings Kremer fed the Nats from the hollow of his hand, but nine men faced him in that time, while the Pirates had again hacked away at Johnson's curves and swifters in the seventh for the two tallies that tied the score.

Peck Does It Again

It was none other than Roger Peckinpaugh who must go down as the "goat" of the series, who contributed predominantly to the Corsair flurry. Peckinpaugh allowed Eddie Moore's high blow back of second base to get away from him and before the ball could be retrieved Moore had anchored on second base. Then and there was the break that swayed the game to Pittsburgh. Carey's third double of the day, a looping fly that fell at Goslin's feet inside the left field foul line, counted Moore and Max lit out for third when Cuyler dumped a nice sacrifice bunt along the first base chalk line.

The second longest hit of the contest followed, a ripping triple into the right center field pocket off Traynor's bat. Carey walked across the plate and Pie, attempting to stretch the hit into a home run, was out on a hairline decision, Ruel taking the ball thrown by Joe Harris and relayed by Stanley Harris just the fraction of a second before the runner.

With the game a deadlock, the crowd lost all semblance of order. Hats, caps, blankets were tossed into the air and on the field, while the Senators coming off the field looked low in spirit, the first time since the series opened.

Like a clap of thunder then came the next scene. Rain was falling steadily and it was so dark that the outfielders could hardly be distinguished against the dark background of the outfield.

Traynor had made a whirl assist on Bluege's skimmer for the first out. Roger Peckinpaugh—the "goat"—was swinging his bat at the plate. There was a sharp crack as bat and ball met—and Roger had hit a homer into the space in front of the scoreboard in left field.

There were those present who saw in Peckinpaugh's hit an attempt by fate to square matters with the battle-scarred veteran. Peck the "bum" was to be made Peck the hero by a single swing of the bat.

The blow gave the Nats a one-run advantage. It was 7 to 6, and the Pirates were coming to bat.

By this time the intensity of the rain had increased and it had grown blacker, a mirror of the Pittsburgh fear as Wright fouled out to Ruel and McInnis lined to Rice.

Smith Starts to Rally

Earl Smith was next. He rammed a double to right field and Manager McKechnie ordered Emil Yde to run for him. Bigbee was sent to the plate to bat for Kremer.

Johnson, meanwhile had asked that sawdust be spread over the pitching mound, by this time a miry sticky spot with secure footing almost impossible. The game was held up while this was done. Bigbee stepped back into the box, there came a fastball, waist high, and Bigbee rattled it against the left field screen for a double, scoring Yde with the run that again tied it up.

Johnson passed Moore and two bases were full when Peckinpaugh, scooping up Carey's roller, threw high to Stanley Harris in an attempt to force Moore at second.

The Hit That Won

And now the blow that won the series.

With two strikes and two balls, Cuyler drove the ball down the right field foul line. It was a double under the ground rules and Bigbee and Moore raced across the plate to the accompaniment of wave upon wave of cheering that was deafening.

Barnhart brought the inning to end by popping to Manager Harris.

With a two-run lead, McKechnie sent Bigbee to left field in Barnhart's place, put John Gooch behind the bat and summoned Rube Oldham, 32-year-old pitcher, who joined the Pittsburgh club late in the season, to the firing line.

Oldham, a lefthander once with Detroit, has a record of defeating the Senators eight consecutive times and yesterday that mark increased to nine.

The veteran faced Rice, Stanley Harris, and Goslin, three of Washington's most dangerous threats.

Rice struck out watching a fast curve pass by without offering at it.

Stanley Harris raised a weak fly, which fell into Eddie Moore's outstretched hands.

Goslin went up. But one putout separated the Pirates from the title.

Foul, strike one. The Goose swung viciously.

Strike two. It was a fast "hook" which fooled the batter completely.

Strike three, a slow curve, which Goslin thought was wide, broke over the plate, and the Pirates were champions.

6

Carnegie Tech's Upset of Notre Dame in a Game Snubbed by Knute Rockne

1926

When undefeated Notre Dame played Carnegie Tech at Forbes Field, its legendary coach Knute Rockne was so confident of victory that he decided to attend the Army-Navy game at Soldier Field instead of traveling to Pittsburgh with his team. It was Notre Dame's next-to-the-last game before heading to the West Coast to play Southern California for the first time. On a cold snowy day, Carnegie Tech, led by All-Americans Lloyd Yoder and Howard Harpster, soundly beat Notre Dame 19–0 in a game that ESPN would rank as the fourth greatest upset in college football history. Carnegie Tech's greatest season was in 1938 when the team finished ranked sixth and went on to an appearance in the Sugar Bowl. Tech also was ranked in 1939, but its college president banned the team from playing in another bowl game.

TECH UPSETS "DOPE," HUMBLES NOTRE DAME

Scarlet-Clad "Under Dogs" Bite out Neat 19-0 Victory

Crowd of 45,000 See Proud Colors of Notre Dame Dragged Down by Fighting Tartans

November 28, 1926
The Pittsburgh Gazette Times

Eleven scarlet-clad Skibos, representing the football team of Carnegie Tech, rose to their greatest heights before a crowd of 45,000 divided partisans at Forbes Field yesterday to spring the biggest upset of the season when they humbled the heretofore undefeated Notre Dame eleven, 19 to 0.

Entering the contest as the proverbial underdog, the view of the brilliant showing of Rockne's famed Riders in previous battles this season, the Tartans exhibited a brand of football that eclipsed anything they have shown and swept their opponents completely off their feet from the first whistle. The Irish, despite the presence of the heralded Four Riders in the backfield, seldom threatened the sacred soil of Coach Steffen's scrappy band of gridiron warriors.

Spectacular Struggle

Those thousands of fans sat through a chilling snowstorm, but it wasn't long until they had forgotten the low temperature. There was too much excitement and brilliant football. They saw the Skibos, a team that had been classed as practically hopeless against Notre Dame, play the greatest game that Pittsburgh has ever seen. They saw the hometown boys trot on the field and excel the Rockne machine in every department of play.

Those thousands were happy in the cold as they saw their favorite lads outpass, outguess, outrun, and play a superior defensive game. Never let it be said that the battle was not decisive. Carnegie deserved to win by just such a margin as it did. If any apologies are to be made, they should come from Notre Dame as a message of gratitude for not having lost by more than 19 points. There are plenty of fans who believe that Field Judge Dan Dougherty robbed the Skibos of one touchdown when he called the ball back after Donohoe had scooped up a fumble and ran 65 yards to cross the goal line.

"But why argue over one touchdown?" said the Plaid boys and they let it go at that.

There were so many of the Tartan stars who played a stellar game that it is hardly fair to single out any few and mark them as superior. The entire eleven men were stars of the first magnitude as they played rings around the highly touted visitors.

To Donohoe, the fast-stepping Carnegie halfback, and Howard Harpster, the midget quarterback, should go perhaps the major portions of the individual glory. The Plaid scored two touchdowns and two field goals. Donohoe scored one of those touchdowns on a beautiful 18-yard end run and Harpster scored both field goals with beautiful dropkicks, one of them from the 41-yard line and the other from the 35-yard line. Both touchdowns were scored in the second quarter while the two field goals were made in the third quarter. A third dropkick was attempted in the fourth period, this one from the 25-yard line, but it was blocked. The other touchdown was scored by Cy Letzelter, the Carnegie fullback.

7

Teddy Yarosz Decisions Vince Dundee for the Middleweight Title

1934

Early in his career, Monaca's Teddy Yarosz was called the "new Pittsburgh windmill," but Yarosz was the opposite of the brawling Harry Greb. Also dubbed "the Polish Kid" and "the Polish Panther," he was once described by a Pittsburgh sportswriter as "a craftsman with the gloves." When he won the middleweight title against Vince Dundee, the fight drew a record 28,000 fans at Forbes Field. Yarosz lost his crown several months later to Babe Risko after suffering a serious knee injury, but he bounced back and eventually fought as a light heavyweight. As a light heavyweight, he defeated Archie Moore and fought three memorable bouts against Billy Conn. Yarosz lost the first two matches on controversial split decisions, but then defeated Conn in their third meeting. One of his last fights was against Ezzard Charles, who would later fight Jersey Joe Walcott at Forbes Field for the heavyweight championship.

YAROSZ WINS MIDDLEWEIGHT TITLE

Split Decision Gives Monacan Crown in Tame 15-Round Battle

28,000 Crowd Sees Teddy Slap Way To Indifferent Triumph; Vince Unimpressive Until Closing Stanzas

September 12, 1934

By Havey J. Boyle

Pittsburgh *Post-Gazette*

The middleweight championship of the world came back to the Pittsburgh district last night at Forbes Field when Ted Yarosz of Monaca won the official decision over Vince Dundee of Newark, the champion, in 15 rounds of as tame fighting as any important championship event ever saw.

It was not a clean-cut victory that Yarosz scored by any means, and he looked unimpressive as he backed away from the champion, scoring his points with light flicking lefts for the most part, and only infrequently opening up with his right hand, and seldom putting on the spurts that twice before accounted for decisions over Dundee.

Officials Disagree

The officials were divided in their opinion, Judge Dr. George McBeth and Al Grayber, the referee, voting for Yarosz, and Judge Leo Houck, of Lancaster, an imported judge, casting his ballot for Dundee. With the judges splitting, the referee had the deciding vote and his vote gave the Monaca boy the championship.

By a slight margin, it seems to this reporter, Yarosz won in the count of rounds, six of them and four for Dundee, with five counted even, but against this count was the fact that the champion did virtually all of the pressing forward as Yarosz circled away and only on one of two occasions did the challenger flash championship stuff in the winning.

Ted Tires at Finish

At the finish it seemed to be a confident, charging Dundee and a Yarosz who seemed a little tired who were winding up as a tame a championship as recent records disclose.

With 28,000 or so fans watching, and most of them, it is fair to assume, partisans of the Pittsburgh district fighter, the lack of enthusiasm was appalling as Yarosz contented himself with flicking light lefts to the jaw and missing an untold number of punches to the body and head.

What saved Yarosz, of course, was that the champion, a veteran with his future behind him, was unimpressive, too, lacking a punch of any power, and fighting a cautious battle until the closing rounds.

Monaca's Teddy Yarosz became the world middleweight champion in 1934 with a 15-round decision over Vince Dundee. (*Post-Gazette* archives)

Neither One Hurt

Not once in the proceedings was either man seriously hurt and both left the ring unmarked, this being due to the light hitting that marked the affair from virtually the beginning to the end. That there was little to choose between them is evidenced by the doubt at the end of at least five of the rounds, resulting in draw verdicts in this account. There were other rounds, too, where a single punch swayed the balance in favor of one man or the others.

With the biggest crowd in the town's history all set to cheer for this home boy, the silence at times was appalling and the suspense as announcer Ray Elberle called for official ballots, to read there from, was an indication of the doubt existing in the minds of the fans. There was no robust or exultant cheering, either, as the popular Yarosz was acclaimed the new champion, for as the fates would have it, they caused him to put up one of his least impressive performances in the big moment.

Cautious at Start

Yarosz, coming in at 157½ pounds, looked fresh and strong, although not completely eager, while Dundee, who enjoyed a spell of success after he had been thought through two years ago, came in at 158½ pounds, looking a little concerned but wearing also a defiant, determined air.

Opening in the fight, both were so cautious that only the light lefts, which were to mark the fight for the most part, set the session apart from a friendly little argument.

Yarosz took up his backing away, flicking a left as he circled backward, while Dundee pursued him, none too viciously, but looking for an opening. Yarosz managed to put in a right hand to the head, but it was not a convincer.

It was in the second that Yarosz gave hopes to his followers that it was going to be a repetition of his first two victories over Dundee when, after starting out tamely, he put on a characteristic spurt, sending in a flurry of strong lefts and a couple of solid rights to Dundee's jaw, which seemed to spell business.

Ted landed one particularly good right hand in this flurry, which slowed up the champion, and Ted won the round with something to spare.

Third Round Even

In the third round there was little done by either boy, Dundee apparently counting himself doing well by bobbing his head like a cork in water as Yarosz missed a series of light lefts to the face and only toward the finish of the round caught Dundee with lefts that carried a little authority. There was so little done, however, by either boy that the round was scored at even.

In the fourth, Yarosz was short with many an attempt to land his left and Dundee was kept so busy avoiding them that he failed to score himself. Yarosz seemed for a second or two to be in for a big moment in this round when he crowded the champion into a neutral corner and, holding him out with his left, prepared to measure him with his right, but the cagy Dundee, whose defense throughout was pretty good, ducked into a clinch and escaped harm. What little was done in the round was done by Yarosz, but that was nothing to write home about.

Vince Makes Ted Miss

In the fifth Dundee had Yarosz missing again and pressing forward. He caught Yarosz with lefts in the head and which made up in number what they lacked in fury. Dundee, a little discouraged, put on a little steam in the following session and was rewarded with finding Ted with his light left hand punch.

Yarosz scored a good right hand to the jaw at the close of this round, making Yarosz miss often and the occasional punches Vince delivered brought him up to even terms with the challenger.

The next round was so tame that neither boy outdistanced the other, light-hitting lefts again marking the session, with Yarosz circling away and Dundee pursuing him but apparently not so eager to catch up with his quarry. Yarosz chanced a few rights and while a couple landed with fair power the boys were pretty much even at the finish.

Teddy Opens Up

Yarosz now came forward with his most consistent drive although it lacked the flavor of his usual medicine, but he managed to find Dundee with enough lefts to roll up sufficient points to capture the eight and ninth rounds. Both boys were on the defense throughout these two sessions with Yarosz winning only because he was less so than his foeman.

The tenth was another tame session and both boys scored about evenly with their indifferent left hands, either to the face or body and after Yarosz managed to eke out a few points, still circling away, with his flicking left halting now and then his retreat.

Many Missed Punches

Dundee evened the score with a left-handed attack. The number of missed punches began to assume by this time, alarming proportions.

Only because Dundee was seemingly satisfied with his progress in defending his title—he had not yet been hurt and was trading light left for light left—did Yarosz manage to scratch out enough points in the eleventh and twelfth rounds to maintain a slight margin over the visitor. In the thirteenth Dundee made his best bid for victory, opening up with two swell rights that caught Yarosz on the jaw and putting more power into his lefts to the head and stomach than he had attempted before. He was rewarded by seeing Yarosz's head bob around a bit after those two rights and he took the round with lots to spare.

The fourteenth was even, lacking, as most of the other rounds, any flashy stuff by either boy, and bringing back the monotonous repetition of light left to the head, another light left to the head, each about breaking even in such exchanges.

Yarosz Begins to Lag

Then in the fifteenth Dundee showed to greater advantage than he had done previously, not because of any particular blows he struck, but because he seemed to have Yarosz by this time out-conditioned. Ted was stumbling awkwardly about in the clinches and some of the extremely optimistic Dundee rooters began calling for a knockout. If Yarosz had gone down, and that did not seem to be even a remote possibility, it would have been though exhaustion coming from missing so many punches and from his continual backward circling.

Dundee was a disappointed boy as the decision was announced and the enthusiasm in Yarosz' corner was not as spontaneous as that which usually marks the winning of a great victory.

Yarosz' dressing room was barred to all but handlers and close friends for quite some time after the fight.

The fight last night was by far the least interesting of the three the boys have now put up.

There were never, it is safe to conjecture, so many silent fans at ringside at there were last night.

It was a very disappointing fight and the explanations from the winning side and the rage of the losing side will be something to look for in the future.

On what they showed neither boy could have complained if the decision went against both, if such a thing were possible.

Vince Complains to Referee

Not a knockdown was scored and the only moment of fighting passion came, to soon pass away, when Dundee complained to Referee Grayber, Yarosz was knocking his punches into foul territory, and another fleeting second when, after Yarosz had struck Dundee when the champion indicated he was set to break clean, the champion shook his head in scorn and considered making it a rough and tumble fight. But he reconsidered and took up the same old pace.

The night was an ideal one for the biggest spectacle in the town's history and Forbes Field was early presented a lively scene as the champion and challenger climbed into the lighted ring to engage in batter.

The fight was handled well by the men in charge and the crowd got a kick out of greeting Jack Dempsey, who refereed two preliminary bouts.

8

Babe Ruth Hits His Last Three Home Runs at Forbes Field

1935

On Saturday, May 25, 1935, Babe Ruth, now 40 years old and days away from his final game as a player, reminded the baseball world of his greatness with an epic performance at Forbes Field. Released by the Yankees in February, Ruth signed a contact with the Boston Braves as a player and assistant manager because he believed the Braves would eventually appoint him as the team's manager. By the end of May, Ruth was struggling at bat and on the field, the Braves were in last place, and management had reneged on its promise to Ruth. After announcing his retirement, Ruth agreed to play on until the Braves completed their first western trip of the season, which included a stop in Pittsburgh. Ruth, in the third game of the series, thrilled the 10,000 fans in attendance by hitting three home runs. His third home run, the last of Ruth's fabled career, cleared the right-field roof, a feat never accomplished before at Forbes Field.

SIDELIGHTS ON SPORTS

May 27, 1935
By Al Abrams
Pittsburgh *Post-Gazette*

What Pirate players said about Babe Ruth's prodigious home run wallops at Forbes Field Saturday:

Manager Pie Traynor: Babe proved to everyone that none can compare with him. Each of his home runs gave me a thrill and a chill at the same time.

Paul Waner: Who said the old Babe can't smack 'em anymore? That second homer must have traveled 450 feet and the third close to 600, if I'm not mistaken.

Hans Wagner: I've seen some great hitters and long distance hits in my day, but none like the Babe's on Saturday. He's the greatest home run hitter of all time.

Coach Jewel Ems: So the Babe's through, eh? He doesn't have to run as long as he smacks 'em like that. Too bad the Braves aren't here today (Sunday) or the fans would be fighting to get into the park.

Red Lucas: The Babe's hard to fool. I knew the instant he took a cut at that ball that she was going to travel. (Babe's first homer was off Lucas.)

Pep Young: Well, he was only two up on me Saturday, but we won't say anything about the distance.

Lloyd Waner: Did you see those balls going? They couldn't have gone any faster or further if they were shot out of a cannon.

Guy Bush: I gave him everything I had with every pitch, but it was the Babe's big day, and when he has 'em there's nothing in the world going to stop him. (Babe's second and third homers were off Guy.)

Tommy Thevenow: Those 10,000 fans that were here Saturday ought to thank their lucky stars for being present. That's one show they'll not soon forget or will never get tired of recalling.

Gus Suhr: I never thought anyone would ever put a ball over the top of the stands in a regular game, but then, I never figured on the Babe.

Woody Jensen: Boy, what a showman! Everything he does has that dramatic flare that only a Ruth can provide.

9

Pitt's John Woodruff Wins 800 Meters Gold Medal in Berlin Olympics

1936

At 6'3", John Woodruff had an awkward running style, but his impressive stride earned him the nickname, "Long John." After graduating from Connellsville High School, Woodruff wanted to follow his idol Jesse Owens to Ohio State, but was talked into attending Pitt. Under the tutelage of the legendary track coach Carl Olson, Woodruff had an outstanding freshman year and qualified for the 1936 Berlin Olympics in the 800 meters. In a dramatic race in which Woodruff had to slow to a momentary stop after being boxed in, he nipped Mario Lanzi of Italy by six-tenths of a second for the gold medal. Woodruff was one of eight African-Americans, mockingly called "the black auxiliaries" by Hitler's regime, to win medals for the United States. After the Olympic games, Woodruff went on to a brilliant track career. When the Penn Relays decided to erect its Wall of Fame, John Woodruff received the most votes for inclusion.

Editor's note: The *Post-Gazette* printed a wire story on the Olympic events. The following story was written from John Woodruff's hometown by a correspondent.

WOODRUFF SUCCESS COMES AFTER SEVERAL SETBACKS

Olympic Champion Fails at Football in High School and in Weight Events Before Finding Specialty

August 5, 1936
By Our Own Correspondent
Pittsburgh Post-Gazette

CONNELLSVILLE, PENNSYLVANIA—August 4—From out of nowhere came Johnny Woodruff of Connellsville to be crowned an Olympic champion today.

Johnny figured in his sophomore year that he would like to be a football player. He reported to the Connellsville High School football squad, but failed to make the team. Then he was persuaded by track coach Joseph Larew to try for a place on the track and field team. Trying the shot put and discus throw, he was a failure.

Finally he was persuaded to attempt a half-mile event. When first invited, he said: "No sir, mister, that's too long." However, in a few short months he had shattered all existing Fayette County high school records in both the half-mile and mile. He tasted defeat only once in his life—in 1934 in the West Virginia University field meet.

His first real sensational showing came in a meet between the Connellsville and Mt. Pleasant high schools. He clearly outdistanced the field. From that time his confidence grew and his time faster until in his senior year in the Connellsville High School, 1935, he was regarded as a human bolt of lightning.

Misfortune befell Johnny during a numbers raid in a Connellsville pool room.

He left his towel there before going to the track and when he dropped in to get it, state troopers swooped down and arrested him with a score of others, engaged in the numbers racket. He later was discharged and thereafter remained away from the pool room.

Johnny is the son of Jacob Woodruff, a WPA worker. His mother and four sisters are the other members of the family.

A movement was started here today to give Woodruff a testimonial on his return here.

JOHN WOODRUFF
GOLD MEDAL—800 METERS
1936 BERLIN OLYMPIC GAMES
BERLIN, GERMANY   Donated by Schieffelin & Somerset Co.

This photo of John Woodruff winning the gold in the 800 meters at the 1936 Berlin Olympic Games hangs in the University of Pittsburgh's Hillman Library. (*Post-Gazette* archives)

10

Pitt's Rose Bowl Victory over Washington and Duquesne's Orange Bowl Victory over Mississippi State

1937

After Pop Warner resigned from Pitt in 1923, he was replaced by Jock Sutherland, an All-American guard on Warner's 1915 and 1916 national champions. The most successful football coach in Pitt's history, Sutherland led his teams to four undefeated seasons and a national championship in 1937, but he couldn't win in the Rose Bowl. After three straight defeats in Pasadena, Pitt, led by Bill Daddio and Marshall Goldberg, finally gained revenge for Sutherland by beating Washington 21–0 in the 1937 Rose Bowl. While Pitt was winning soundly in the Rose Bowl, Clipper Smith's Duquesne Dukes, the only team to defeat Pitt during the season, were winning a thriller in the Orange Bowl against Mississippi State. With time running out, Boyd Brumbaugh threw a 52-yard touchdown pass to Ernie Hefferle to give Duquesne a 13–12 comeback victory. Brumbaugh, the hero of the 1937 Orange Bowl, went on to play for the Pittsburgh Steelers.

THE PANTHERS COME THROUGH

January 3, 1937
By Havey Boyle
Pittsburgh Post-Gazette

It was a long wait, but the Panthers of Pitt finally got revenge for three Rose Bowl beatings when they took the famed Washington Huskies over the jumps for a 21 to 0 victory, which probably helped convince some of the Coast boys that, after all, the Panthers saw a football before they visited the Coast.

To the Pitt line must go the biggest end of the credit for they displayed their power offensively and bottled up the Washington attack in a way that caused the Huskies to resort steadily and dangerously to the air.

The Pitt ends helped check the noteworthy passing attack of the Huskies, Daddio and Hoffman rushing in to hurry the passers, with Daddio coming out of the battle as the individual hero. He scored enough points himself to win the game, what with his touchdown run, for 70 yards, after he had intercepted a pass, and his three placements for a total of nine points for the afternoon.

Frank Patrick and Bobby LaRue furnished the speed and power in carrying the ball and Marshall Goldberg distinguished himself in the role of blocker to pave the way for his backfield mates. Concentrating on stopping the mad attack of Goldberg, Washington found their chief worries coming from two other guys, as Goldberg knocked out the ends and the secondary.

That it took the best Pitt had to stop the passing of the Huskies was shown by the way the Coast team started going to town with the Pitt second stringers in. They moved from their own 10 down to the Pitt 30 in a series of passes, which prompted Dr. Sutherland to take no further liberties with the Huskies. He sent back the old trusties and the Washington attack immediately did a fold up.

Pitt lived up to its reputation as a power machine and a great defensive unit. They defeated the Huskies worse than the Minnesota team, which defeated Washington 14 to 7.

Perhaps in the future the Coast boys won't be so certain that Pitt is just another "el foldo," as the Coast boys said.

Two Duke Heroes

Urban Brumbaugh took on the color of a Dick Merriwell yesterday in helping Duquesne to overcome what seemed to be certain defeat in the thriller down Miami way against Mississippi State. While the Southerners got their second touchdown a moment or so after Brumbaugh went into the game in the second quarter, it was not long after that the Dukes scored their first touchdown. Brumbaugh and Matsik conducted a joint tour to the goal line shortly after the kickoff following the Southerners' second touchdown. The two backs passed and ran their way to the 1-yard line. Momentarily, the Southerners stiffened and held Brumbaugh as he tried a plunge through center, but on the next play the Duke ace hit guard and rolled over the line. He followed this by kicking the extra point.

The fact that Brumbaugh virtually got out of a sick bed to take his part in the intersectional contest added luster to his performance, and then in true Merriwell fashion in the fourth quarter with the game passing into its final stages and with the ball deep in Duquesne territory, Brumbaugh once again took part in a touchdown.

The last touchdown effort by the Dukes started on their own 10-yard line. Pickle punted and Brumbaugh moved the ball forward five yards when he was stopped on the Duquesne 15. Matsik could make no ground around right end, and on the next play Brumbaugh passed to Platukis, who moved to the Duquesne 28. Once again, the accurate Brumbaugh tossed one—this time to Hefferle who caught it on the Mississippi 30, and ran for a touchdown. Brumbaugh's second try for the point after touchdown failed, but the Dukes were ahead 13 to 12 by this time and the game was pretty well in the bag, as there was time left for only a few more plays.

Hefferle and Brumbaugh by their work yesterday cut themselves a niche in the Duke hall of fame set apart for Dukemen who pull games out of the fire in the closing moments of play.

Billy Conn Decisions Melio Bettina for Light-Heavyweight Title

1939

After spending his childhood on the mean streets of East Liberty, Billy Conn became a professional boxer when he was still a teenager. Fighting as a welterweight, he struggled early, barely winning more than half of his fights, but as he moved up in weight he became more and more successful in the ring. As a middleweight, he fought and defeated Teddy Yarosz, Fritzie Zivic, and Tony Zale before advancing to the light-heavyweight division, where he became world champion in 1939. After two years, he vacated his crown and moved up to the heavyweight division. In one of the most memorable fights in boxing history, Conn met Joe Louis in June 1941 and had Louis defeated until he was knocked out in the unlucky 13th round. With his East Liberty background and Hollywood looks, Conn was one of the most popular figures in Pittsburgh sports history.

CONN'S VICTORY CLIMAXES SHORT BUT BRILLIANT CAREER

East Liberty Youth Wins Light-Heavyweight Title in Fifty-Second Bout; Started in 1935, Never Fought as Amateur

July 14, 1939
By Jack Sell
Pittsburgh Post-Gazette

Young Billy Conn's victory over Southpaw Melio Bettina last night in Madison Square Garden climaxed a storybook career which has seen the East Liberty lad clamber from the crowded ranks of preliminary boys to the world's light-heavyweight championship within a space of five years. Only 21 years of age, the youngster this morning looks forward to still greater honors, with the biggest bauble of them all, the world's heavyweight crown, as the goal of future ring efforts.

The record books show Conn to have crawled through the ropes exactly 52 times, including last night's crucial engagement. He has never been kayoed but has dropped seven decisions. All the other times he wended his way back to the dressing room triumphant.

Has Scored Seven Kayos

Billy is not a slugger type and only seven times has he sent his rivals to dreamland. He has strung out a total of 38 decisions. No less than 12 times he has traded swings with champions or former champions and on nine occasions he came off the winner. However, up until last night he never had an opportunity to grab a crown.

While most mitt stars go through an apprenticeship in the amateur ranks, Conn never tossed punches for a merchandise certificate or the inevitable timepiece. He took his lesson from Johnny Ray, masterful lightweight ringman, and when his tutor felt the time was right, Billy went to the ring wars for the first time in 1935. His development was rapid but it was not until early this year when he crashed the big time in New York against Fred Apostoli that he vaulted into the national spotlight.

Has Met Many Champs

Previously Billy had mingled with numerous champs and ex-champs. He split even in two bouts with Young Corbett, ex-welter titlist; he copped two out of three from Teddy Yarosz, former middleweight leader; he decisioned Vince Dundee and Babe Risko, other recent middleweight kings. Solly Krieger, later to gain the middleweight diadem, beat Billy in 1937 but had the tables turned here in 1938.

With his impressive record against high-class opposition, Conn made his debut in Madison Square Garden last January 6 against Fred Apostoli, a coast slugger who was recognized in New York and California as middleweight title-holder. The local lad was the underdog but

Pittsburgh boxing great Billy Conn won the light-heavyweight title in 1939. (*Post-Gazette* archives)

he surprised everyone with a 10-round decision. A rematch was in order and they met again on February 10 in the same ring. This time the distance was 15 rounds and because Billy had showed signs of weakening near the finish in their first fight, Apostoli again was favored. Billy paced himself, however, and at the end of the long grind once more received the duke.

Since that time he has fought only twice, romping to an easy decision over Solly Krieger in 12 rounds and then downing Bettina last night for a clean sweep of four straight starts in Madison Square Garden.

Billy Soose Defeats Ken Overlin for Middleweight Title

1941

With the popularity of Billy Conn, it's easy to overlook the accomplishments of his contemporary, Farrell's Billy Soose. When a biography of Soose was published, its title was *The Champion Time Forgot.* But Soose became one of the most successful amateur fighters in boxing history and, despite damaging a tendon in his right hand in only his sixth professional match, went on to win the middleweight title. As an amateur, Soose won three Golden Gloves and, after accepting a scholarship at Penn State, became an intercollegiate boxing champion. He was so dominant in college that officials decided to ban boxers who had fought in the Golden Gloves. After defeating Tony Zale and Kenny Overlin within 30 days, Soose was declared "an uncrowned champion." He claimed the crown a few months later by defeating Overlin for the middleweight title. He gave up the title to fight as a light heavyweight, but never fought again after serving in World War II.

Editors' note: Uncertain words in the following story, illegible in the archived copy of the article, are marked with ellipses.

SOOSE DEFEATS OVERLIN, WINS TITLE

Unanimous Decision Is Given Bill

Verdict Stuns Fans as Vet Appears Far in Front

May 10, 1941
By Havey Boyle
Pittsburgh Post-Gazette

NEW YORK—May 9—A third world's boxing championship went to Western Pennsylvania tonight when Billy Soose, Penn State's product, and Farrrell, PA, native, was voted the middleweight king after 15 rounds of lively fighting against Ken Overlin, former gob of Norfolk, in Madison Square Garden.

Soose joins Fritzie Zivic, the welter champ, and Billy Conn, undefeated light-heavyweight, in the ranks of the soft coal boys who rule their respective roosts in the fighting coop.

The crowd of 11,614 paid a net of $35,973 to see the show.

Decision Surprises

The decision was greeted with a lusty round of boos from the fans with astonishment written on the faces of the ringside kibitzers and not without a tinge of surprise from the Farrell boy himself. Before the decision was announced, it seemed to the ticket holders up front that Soose's only chance to win the first few rounds was to either knock out Overlin or hire an expert boxer.

Curiously, in the face of the rather general sentiment that Overlin had won, the entire panel of official jurors cast its vote for Soose, thus adding to the general amazement. To boot, the third man in the ring was the reliable and forthright Arthur Donovan, who voted with the sideline judges.

Overlin Seems Winner

Always making allowances for a difference of opinion in such cases, this one seemed to be actually a one-sided victory by Overlin and adding to this

Billy Soose (left) battles for the middleweight crown during his 1941 bout with Ken Overlin. (*Post-Gazette* archives)

impression were the somewhat frantic efforts of Soose in the last round to go all out in order to achieve a knockout that might salvage what seemed to be certain defeat.

Unless the officials scored extra heavily for Soose's steady advance...the decision must stand as one of the incongruous that a middleweight title fight has ever seen.

Except for a brief span in the eighth, ninth, and tenth rounds, two of which Soose won clearly and decisively because he seemed to have the champion in a little trouble in the ninth and tenth, Overlin seemed here to be far out in front most of the way.

While he never had Soose in danger, he piled up point after point, cracking steadily to Billy's stomach with a left hook, maneuvering the challenger out of position time after time to follow up with one-two belts to the head,

Middleweight boxing champion Billy Soose, from Farrell, Pennsylvania. (*Post-Gazette* archives)

and steadily frustrating the Farrell, Pennsylvania, boy in the various phases of fighting.

Overlin had nothing in his right hand to bother the tall challenger, but he belted Soose so often with a left hook that moved now to the chin, and then to the basement, that there seemed to be no question in the minds of ringsiders as to who was the top man at the finish.

Billy Has Flurry

Soose's chief moment of glory, aside from the very satisfying verdict, came in the ninth and tenth rounds when he found the range for a while with right hand shots that put Overlin in temporary trouble, but the champ had enough savvy to fox himself out of danger. Soose was picking up a little ground in the latter half of the fight, but Overlin always had enough to stave off a Soose rally and enough to give him the edge, even while Soose was trying so eagerly after he found the range for a short time in the ninth and tenth here.

There was not a knockdown in the fight and neither boy was suffering from any serious marks at the finish, but from the standpoint of the heaviest and most consistent punching, Overlin seemed to have this one well in hand.

To Soose's credit it must be said he never gave up, never yielded ground. He always seemed to be more eager to keep up a steady and fast pace, but Overlin had the challenger fighting just about the way that suited the veteran's purpose.

Overlin would countercharge from a retreat and belt pretty hooks into the stomach and when this attack led him into close quarters, he fumbled and held while Soose tried in vain to test out his infighting. In short, Overlin scored best at long range, where Soose was weakest and checked the challenger where apparently Soose was the better because he was fresher and stronger.

It was a crestfallen champion who heard the title being announced away, after he had put up a swell, smart fight, and of course, it was elated Soose who bounced around when he was called the winner. Just a moment before Soose was throwing caution to the winds in an effort to land a kayo blow and there was in his actions the imprint of a loser.

Nothing but a new chance will satisfy Overlin's rooters and likely they will be accommodated.

13

Billy Conn Loses Heavyweight Title Fight against Joe Louis

1941

In 1936, Billy Conn won a controversial decision over Fritzie Zivic in a match that was suppose to be friendly but turned into a brawl. Four years after the fight, "the Croatian Comet," Fritzie Zivic, regarded in his day as one of the dirtiest fighters in the game, won the welterweight title by defeating Henry Armstrong at Madison Square Garden. Less than a year later, Zivic's fellow Pittsburgher, Billy Conn, after winning the light-heavyweight title, moved up to the heavyweight division to challenge Joe Louis and put himself in a position to pull off the greatest boxing upset since Gentleman Jim Corbett defeated the great John L. Sullivan. When Zivic fought Conn, he praised Conn as a smart fighter but said, "He couldn't knock your hat off." On June 18, 1941, Conn outsmarted Joe Louis until the 13th round when, ahead on points, he decided to go for a knockout. It turned into the dumbest move of Conn's boxing career and made a prophet of Fritzie Zivic.

Editors' note: Uncertain words in the following story, illegible in the archived copy of the article, are marked with ellipses.

LOUIS WINS IN 13TH OVER BILLY CONN

54,487 See Local Lad Falter After Fine Ring Showing

Far Ahead on Points

Crown Almost in Grasp When Brown Bomber Finds Range

June 19, 1941
By Havey Boyle
Pittsburgh Post-Gazette

NEW YORK—June 18—Within a few brief seconds after he seemed to be on his way to winning the heavyweight championship, Billy Conn, Pittsburgh's entry in the top division of fighting, was stretched on his side of the ring floor, the knockout victim of a furious onslaught by Joe Louis in the Polo Grounds here tonight.

The Pittsburgh boy went down fighting gallantly and throwing back punches almost to the very end, but he could not withstand the powerful series of lefts and rights that Louis poured out to his chin and body in the final round.

The end came after two minutes and 58 seconds in the thirteenth with Conn just about rising at the count of it, but plainly weak and battered. The referee finished his count and then led Conn to his corner.

Takes Many Punches

Until Louis brought the flurry of blows that brought the end, Conn was doing well. In fact, he seemed to be improving with every round, but he made the fatal error of meeting Louis on Louis' terms and the furious exchanges between the two men earlier in the thirteenth had left Conn tired and unable to move swiftly or to block Louis' relentless two-handed attack. Conn must have been hit 20 times by the champion in the final series of the bout and the last two, a left and a right, put the Pittsburgher down.

It marked the initial time in the loser's brilliant career that he suffered a knockout defeat.

Fifty-four thousand four hundred and eight-seven fans, including about 3,000 from Western Pennsylvania, paid a gross gate of … and were thrilled by the winning climax and the events immediately preceding the knockout.

Coming from behind after the ninth round, Conn was outpointing the champion up to the thirteenth, not only outpointing him, but actually putting Louis in distress in the twelfth round with a two-handed attack that not only had the champion bewildered, but showing signs that he was being hurt.

Success Brings Downfall

In fact, it might have been Conn's glittering success with his left hand to the jaw, his right crosses, his hold punching—pulling Louis into him with his left and marking in a right to the body—and a whole assortment of punches that led, ironically, to Conn's downfall.

Feeling that Louis was weakening under the twelfth round barrage, Conn came out in the thirteenth refusing to resume the dancing and sparring that had marked most of the early rounds, and instead stood flat footed and returned blow for blow as Louis punched with short but powerful blows to the head and body.

14

Hornets Win
First Calder Cup

1952

Pittsburgh played a major role in the early years of professional hockey and, by 1925, gained a franchise in the National Hockey League. The Pittsburgh Pirates, playing at an undersized and dilapidated Duquesne Gardens, struggled financially, and at the end of the 1929–1930 season, finally left town and became the Philadelphia Quakers. For the 1935–1936 season, theatre magnate John Harris bought the Detroit Olympics in the minor-league American Hockey League and moved the franchise to Pittsburgh, where they became the Hornets. Affiliated with the Toronto Maple Leafs, the Hornets sent future Hall-of-Famers, like George Armstrong and Tim Horton, to the NHL. After losing three Calder Cup finals, the franchise won its first championship in 1952 against the Providence Reds. The team was led by Tim Horton, Frank Mather, one of the greatest defensemen in AHL history, and goalie Gil "the Needle" Mayer.

HORNETS WIN IN SUDDEN DEATH, 3–2

R. Hannigan Sinks Reds in Cup Final

Clincher Comes at 6:08 Mark in Second Overtime

April 21, 1952
By Jimmy Jordan
Pittsburgh Post-Gazette

PROVIDENCE, RHODE ISLAND—April 20—Ray Hannigan, Pittsburgh left wing, slapped the puck 15 feet into the Providence net in the second overtime period here tonight. And on that shot rode the first Calder Cup the Hornets ever won in 16 seasons in the American Hockey League.

A screaming crowd of 6,154, largest in three seasons in the Auditorium here, groaned as the shot flashed past Goalie Harvey Bennett to end the game at 6:08 of the "sudden death" period.

The Providence team, a nemesis to the Hornets for several seasons, had rallied twice in the second period to tie the score, and at the end of regulation time the count was 2–2. After a 10-minute overtime period, which was scoreless, an intermission was taken before the sudden death overtime.

Close-Checking Game

After six minutes and eight seconds of milling, in which there were few scoring threats, Hannigan took a pass from Chuck Blair and blasted it past Bennett to wind up the season.

Conspicuous by his absence was league president Maurice Podoloff. Neither Podoloff nor the Calder Cup were present at the playoff game. Just when the cup will be presented still was a mystery after it had been won by the Hornets.

The game was a close-checking affair all the way, with the both clubs having 37 shots on the goal and with Pittsburgh having the advantage of Hannigan's overtime shot which spelled the difference.

Fourth Overtime Battle

The game followed almost the same pattern as last week's 3–2 victory on the same ice, in which Rudy Migay, limping on a crippled left knee, slammed the same kind of shot past Bennett at 18:40 of the second overtime period.

The Hornets battled through two overtime games with Hershey in the first playoff series. And this was their second overtime game in the Providence series.

Last season the Hornets battled Cleveland into the seventh game before surrendering hope for the Calder Cup by a 3–1 decision. That was the third time they had come within one game of winning it. They finally made it the fourth time.

Barbe Gets First Goal

The line of Barbe, Migay, and Solinger, which was responsible for more than half of the scoring in the first five games of the title series, came through with the first goal of the game after a minute and nine seconds of play, with Barbe smashing a waist-high shot past Goalie Bennett from 30 feet out.

Providence tied the count after but 16 seconds of play in the second period, when Sullivan's 20-foot shot bounced over Mayer's skate and into the net. Boivin, who had drawn a penalty for elbowing just before the end of the first period, was in the bastille at the time.

Horton put the Hornets back in front at 9:07 of the period when he stole the puck from Lund at mid-ice and skated in for an unassisted tally from the left side of the net.

Hassard scored an apparent goal at 14:35 of the period, but referee Frank Udvari ruled that he had kicked the puck in and the goal was disallowed. Ezinicki was banished for 10 minutes on a misconduct penalty in an ensuing argument.

K. Smith, a former Hornet, tied the score again at 18:46 of the period when he took a pass from Toppazzini and skated from mid-ice to beat Mayer with a short shot from the left side.

Hassard, Solinger, and Ezinicki all had good shots stopped by Bennett before they went into overtime for the second time in the series.

After a scoreless 10-minute overtime period, Ray Hannigan ended the series with a 15-foot shot into the left-hand corner of the net, which brought the Hornets their first Calder Cup in their 16 seasons in the American Hockey League. He had taken a pass from Chuck Blair near the blue line and skated on in to catch Goalie Bennett off guard for the clincher.

15

Ralph Kiner Hits 37th Home Run to Clinch Seventh Consecutive Home Run Title

1952

One of the most prolific sluggers in baseball history, Ralph Kiner had the misfortune of playing on some of the worst teams in Pirates history. In the early 1950s, the only thing that kept Pirate fans at Forbes Field in the late innings was the chance to see Kiner hit one of his towering home runs. From his rookie season in 1946 to his last full season with the Pirates in 1952, Kiner either led or tied for the lead in home runs in the National League. In 1954, he challenged Hack Wilson's National League home run record (since shattered by Mark McGwire and Barry Bonds) of 56 before finally ending the season with 54 home runs. A California native, he was a glamour boy (he once dated Elizabeth Taylor) in the Smoky City. Pirate fans were stunned and never forgave Branch Rickey for trading Kiner to the Chicago Cubs during the 1953 season. Kiner was elected to the Baseball Hall of Fame in 1975, his last year of eligibility.

KINER LEADS OR TIES 7TH TIME

Major Record

September 29, 1952
By Dan McGibbeny
Pittsburgh Post-Gazette

Time almost ran out on Ralph Kiner. But the Pirate home run slugger managed to beat the deadline as he once again wrote his name in the major league record book.

By hitting his 37th home run Saturday to deadlock Chicago Cub outfielder Hank Sauer for the 1952 championship, Kiner became the first player in major league history to win or tie for the top spot seven straight seasons.

Kiner also broke a National League record for winning or tying for the home run title for the seventh time. He had shared the distinction of winning six titles with Mel Ott, former New York Giant outfielder, and Clifford (Gabby) Cravath, former Philadelphia Phillie outfielder.

Ironically, Kiner's 37th home run this season was blasted at Crosley Field in Cincinnati, where he has socked only eight in the seven seasons since he joined the Pirates in 1946.

The home run, struck off Red pitcher Bubba Church with two on base Saturday, also enabled Kiner to complete the cycle of connecting for a round-tripper in every National League park. He has turned that trick five times in seven seasons. He was shut out at Crosley Field both times in which he failed.

Of the 37 home runs hit by Kiner and Sauer, each smashed 22 in their home parks and 15 on the road. Kiner also collected five at St. Louis, three at New York, three at Boston, and one each at Brooklyn, Philadelphia, and Chicago.

Kiner has hit 294 home runs in the seven seasons, belting 171 at Forbes Field and 123 on the road. Away from home, he has hit 23 at Brooklyn, 23 at Chicago, 19 at St. Louis, 18 at Boston, 16 at New York, 16 at Philadelphia, and eight at Cincinnati.

Boston pitchers yielded seven this season. Off other clubs, he collected six each from the Giants and the Cards, five each from the Dodgers, Phils and Cubs, and three from the Reds.

He hit one home run in April, five in May, six in June, eight in July, ten in August, and seven in September.

Ironically, he shared the lead only twice during the season on opening day and the next-to-last day.

Ralph Kiner (right) of the Pittsburgh Pirates and Gil Hodges of the Brooklyn Dodgers at Forbes Field. (Morris Berman/*Post-Gazette*)

16

Steelers Win Revenge Match against the Philadelphia Eagles

1954

The Pittsburgh Steelers gave fans little to cheer about in their early history. There were Art Rooney's Same Old Steelers, a predictable and mediocre team of misfits and has-beens usually coached by one of Rooney's cronies. But within a two-week span at Forbes Field in 1954, the Steelers were remarkable. First they crushed the Cleveland Browns 55–27 for their first win in team history over Paul Brown's perennial champions. Six days later, they met their cross-state rivals, the Philadelphia Eagles, in a grudge match after a controversial loss in Philadelphia a few weeks earlier. The Steelers-Eagles games were usually blood baths, and this game was no exception. With quarterback Jimmy Finks wearing a catcher's mask on his helmet to protect a broken jaw and split end Elbie Nickel leading the way, the Steelers defeated the Eagles in arguably the greatest win in the team's pre-Super Bowl history.

ELBIE NICKEL CALLED PLAY THAT BEAT EAGLES

52-yard TD Pass Proved Decisive

Coach Kiesling Credits Co-Captain with Plotting Dangerous Strategy

October 25, 1954
By Jack Sell
Pittsburgh Post-Gazette

The Pittsburgh Steelers not only ended a three-year jinx by beating the Philadelphia Eagles 17–7 last Saturday night in Forbes Field. They also convinced the most skeptical fan that they really have championship class this season.

Many of the 39,075, exactly 15 over the previous record attendance, were ready with the annual wail of "Same Old Steelers." But Coach Walter Kiesling's protégés took a 3–0 lead in the second quarter on a 24-yard field goal by Ed Kissell and stayed in front the rest of the distance.

Brandt Used as Decoy

The big play came at 6:25 of the third quarter. It was third and 1 on the Steeler 48. Let Kiesling take it from there.

"There was a timeout and Elbie Nickel suggested a pass," Kies said last night. "He figured he could get loose and catch the Eagles napping. Jimmy Finks was doubtful, pointing out it was very dangerous. But I told him to go ahead and gamble.

"I sent in Jim Brandt to help confuse the Eagles. He usually carried for short yardages. Finks took the ball from Walsh, faked a handoff to Rogel and stepped back. No one paid any attention to Elbie and he was out in the clear, a perfect target for Jimmy. Nickel gets the credit for it all."

There was considerable confusion in the press box about who kicked the extra point. Some credited Paul Held, who has been handling that department.

"It was Kissell who made both conversions," Kiesling advised. "Held and Dewey McConnell didn't get into the game at all."

Coach Jim Trimble's invaders got into contention at 3:32 of the final quarter when Adrian Burk passed 24 yards to end Pete Pihos in the end zone and Bobby Walston converted.

Kies Gives Boys Vacation

That didn't bother the locals who proceeded to go for a second TD of their own. Lynn Chandnois circled his own left end from five yards out for the six points at 9:39.

Kiesling rewarded his protégés for their great showing in the past two games by calling off practice until Wednesday. He feels a rest cure is just the ticket for the squad, which has been under heavy pressure.

Fullback Fran Rogel, who led the Steeler runners with 38 yards against the Eagles, will have a bruised leg X-rayed this morning. Guard John Schweder, with a pulled leg muscle, is the only other causality.

Bill McPeak, veteran right end, started against the Birds on defense despite a sprained ankle. When Kiesling saw that the ex-Pitt star was unable to maneuver properly, he sent in Rookie Joe Zombek, a Panther last season, and the youngster made an excellent showing.

Next foe is the winless Chicago Cardinals in Comiskey Park next Sunday afternoon.

The Eagles and New York Giants, tied with the Steelers in the Eastern Conference with 4–1 records, may have their troubles this weekend.

The Green Bay Packers, victorious in their last two starts, invade Connie Mack Stadium on Saturday night while the Maramen have a date in Cleveland with the Browns on Sunday afternoon.

17

Duquesne Defeats Dayton, Wins NIT

1955

In Pittsburgh sports history, the Duquesne Dukes, under Chick Davies and Dudey Moore, were to college basketball what the Pitt Panthers, under Pop Warner and Jock Sutherland, were to college football. After Davies' arrival in 1924, the Dukes became a national powerhouse and appeared regularly in the NIT and NCAA tournaments (teams could play in both in those days). When Moore replaced Davies, he continued the winning tradition and led the top-ranked Dukes into the 1955 NIT where they played the sixth-ranked Dayton Flyers. In that game, All-Americans Dick Ricketts and Si Green scored all 35 of Duquesne's first-half points. Green scored 33 and Ricketts 22 points for the game as the Dukes defeated Dayton 70–58. Ricketts and Green became the first players from the same team to be the top pick in the NBA draft in consecutive years. In 1950, the Dukes' All-American Chuck Cooper had become the first African-American selected in the NBA draft.

5,000 GREET CHAMPION DUKE TEAM

Rally Scheduled On Campus Today For Champions

March 21, 1955
By Alvin Rosensweet
Pittsburgh Post-Gazette

Duquesne's conquering Dukes, champions of all they surveyed in the National Invitation Tournament in New York, flew home yesterday to a rousing welcome that ranged from Greater Pittsburgh Airport to the Bluff.

More than 5,000 persons broke into the airport landing field to get a close-up of Dudey Moore, Si Green, and their scoring machine. Thousands more craned their necks from the airport windows and the observation deck, then joined a horn-tooting motorcade that brought the NIT champions to Downtown and broke the Sunday quiet.

Campus Rally Today

And yesterday's homecoming looked like only a prelude of more to come. Duke students will rally on the campus at 9 o'clock this morning and Father Vernon F. Gallagher promised a celebration at South Park this afternoon. It's a reasonably good guess that it will be hard to round-up a quorum for classes all day.

Yesterday's throng gaped and gawked at the champs, but mostly at Sihugo Green, the human jumping jack, who scored 33 points against the University of Dayton in Saturday night's 79–58 finale. But the crowd had a full-length, six-six disappointment, too.

"Where's Dick Ricketts?" they asked as one player after another got off the plane.

On Way to Kansas City

But the plane failed to deliver the other half of the Duquesne scoring twins. Ricketts was on his way to Kansas City for the East-West Game.

So the crowd lavished its attention mostly on Green, although reserving cheers, too, for the younger Ricketts, Dave; Mickey Winograd, Jim Fallon, and the other Duquesne champions.

It was Green whom the autograph-seekers besieged as he rode in the back of a red convertible with Dudey Moore and Mrs. Moore. It was Green who caught the fancy of the youngsters. They watched him with wonder in their eyes and a shaver about nine years old said to his buddies on the Bluff:

"Let's go follow Green."

And it was Green who voiced the way the Dukes felt about the big welcome home party when he said:

"This is wonderful. I never expected anything like it."

The crowd at the airport jammed the ramp an hour before the Dukes were due to arrive on Capital flight 471 at 1:07 PM. Cameras and homemade signs were plentiful. Some read "Welcome Home Dukes," and one, a reproach of Dayton's seven-foot center, said: "Uhl never had it so good."

Sergeant E. J. Andrews and the detail of Allegheny County police didn't have a chance to hold back the crowd once the plane landed.

Seven bright and shiny cars were waiting for the Dukes and hundreds of motorists joined the procession. A city motorcycle, sent out for escort duty, broke down on the way to the Airport, so the motorcade made it alone, scooting through the red lights on Grant Street, Liberty Avenue, Fifth Avenue, then up steep Shingiss Street to the campus.

There the neighbors joined the crowd and set off a second demonstration at Colbert and Vickroy streets in front of Canevin Hall.

It was no place for a boy from Dayton, and that's just where this reporter is from!

18

Hornets Win Second Calder Cup

1955

After winning their first Calder Cup in 1952, the Hornets lost to the Cleveland Barons in the finals the following year on a freak goal. They were back in 1955, and this time defeated the Buffalo Bisons for their second Calder Cup. Defenseman Frank Mathers and goalie Gil Mayer were still with Hornets, but the outstanding player in the 1954–1955 season was Willie Marshall. He led the Hornets in scoring and was the MVP in the Calder Cup final. Marshall went on to become the greatest scorer in AHL history. Mather, Mayer, and Marshall were eventually elected to the AHL Hall of Fame. The Hornets played one more season in Pittsburgh before being disbanded after the Duquesne Gardens were torn down. When the Civic Arena opened, the Hornets franchise returned to Pittsburgh and won its third Calder Cup in 1965 under the leadership of Baz Bastien.

HORNETS WIN, 4–2; REGAIN AHL'S CALDER CUP

Buffalo Battles To Bitter End

Bison Pull Goalie in Final Minute, Score, Yield Goal

April 11, 1955
By Jimmy Jordan
Pittsburgh Post-Gazette

BUFFALO—April 10—The Hornets will return the Calder Cup, the emblem of American Hockey supremacy, to The Gardens in Pittsburgh tomorrow.

They won it here tonight by beating Buffalo, 4–2, in a rough and at times ragged game which turned into veritable bedlam in the closing minute as the partisan crowd of 7,419 fans in the Memorial Auditorium howled themselves hoarse when their Bisons came within inches of tying the count.

Wasp Scores Three in Second

Actually, the Hornets won the game—and the cup—in the second period, when they scored three quick goals, the first by Ray Timgren and the next two by Bob Solinger.

But when Buffalo scored two goals late in the final period, and continued an almost unending assault of Hornet goalie Gil Mayer, it appeared there could be a repetition of Saturday night's game at The Gardens where the Bisons won in overtime 5–4.

Kenny Wharram, the villain of that piece, scored for Buffalo at 13:03. With little more than a minute of play remaining, coach Gaye Stewart removed goalie Ray Frederick for a power play, and it paid off immediately. Frank Sullivan, a former Hornet, made it 3–2 with a short shot at 19:08.

Marshall Gets Clincher

The clincher came at 19:37 when Willie Marshall and Earl Balfour broke loose following a faceoff on the Hornet end of the ice and skated down to the unprotected Buffalo goal. Balfour flipped the puck to Marshall, who easily dunked it into the net, and the Calder Cup went to the Hornets.

The Hornets won all three of the games they played on Buffalo ice, and won the big trophy for only the second time since they entered the AHL, four games to two. Conversely, the two games they lost were both at The Gardens.

They beat Buffalo by scores of 5–4, 4–3 and 3–2, in addition to tonight's win, while losing at home 3–1, and 5–4, the latter in the only overtime of the final series.

But while the now-silent, disconsolate crowd was filing out of the Auditorium, there was another bedlam under way in the Hornet clubhouse as the players whooped it up, congratulated each other, and in general released the pent-up tensions of the series.

Buffalo Clubhouse Quiet

It was, naturally, a different picture in the Bison clubhouse. The players who rallied from almost certain defeat to win Saturday night's game and keep their title hopes alive, sat quietly in front of their lockers for the most part, resting and replaying the game in which they lost all chance for the playoff mug.

Coach Gaye Stewart, far from gay at the time, had no alibis to offer.

"We made mistakes in that second period and we got into trouble," he said. "It was a good series, and but for that one lapse we might be going back to Pittsburgh for a seventh game."

Freshman Coach Howie Meeker was, naturally, in a much different mood than on Saturday night, but he had little to say.

"They played good hockey and won. Every one of them. What more is there to say. They played hard all season and they deserved it. I'm proud to have coached them. And I hope we can do it again next season."

Meeker's victory duplicates that of coach King Clancy three years ago. It was Clancy's first season with the Hornets and he won both the regular season and championship in the Calder Cup. Meeker did the same in his first season. Those two titles and those two cups are the only ones ever won by Hornet teams.

The Hornets left by plane for Pittsburgh shortly after the game. A victory celebration was planned at The Gardens in the wee hours of Monday morning.

Gang Up on Mayer

The Bisons gave Mayer a tough time in the first period as they worked in for close shots. Twice he was down on the ice, the second time after he had lost his stick and a glove, but with some help from his mates he managed to keep the puck out of the cage.

Timgren scored the first goal of the game for the Hornets at 6:09 of the second period. Following a faceoff at the blue line, he stole the puck from Pilote in the faceoff circle to the left of the cage and fired a 12-foot angle shot past Frederick.

Three minutes later at 9:33, Solinger made it 2–0 for the Hornets. Andy Barbe grabbed the puck, also on the left, and skated down the lane. Passed across to Solinger, who was steaming down the middle. Solly fired a point blank blast into the cage.

Then the Wasps made it 3–0 with Solinger again scoring at 12:35. This time he was skating down the right lane and took a pass from Marshall. He fired at an almost impossible angle from 15 feet out, but it went in for the clincher.

Bisons Battle to End

The Bisons finally broke into the scoring column at 13:03 of the final stanza when Wharram, who had scored the game-winning overtime goal at Pittsburgh Saturday night, broke loose from center ice to tally.

Buffalo added another at 19:08, a few seconds after Frederick was taken from the nets for a power attack. Frank Sullivan, a former Hornet, tallied the counter, with assists from Wharram and Babando.

The Hornets got another at 19:37 when Marshall and Balfour broke loose from their own defensive zone and went down to score easily as the goal was unprotected. Balfour passed across the ice to Marshall, who barged home the insurance shot.

19

Dale Long Hits Home Run in Eighth Consecutive Game

1956

If Branch Rickey had his way, rookie Dale Long would have made baseball history in 1951 by becoming a left-handed catcher. But the spring training experiment failed, and Long was sent back to the minors. He wouldn't play his first full major league season until 1955. A year later, in 1956, Long did make baseball history by hitting home runs in eight consecutive games, something that had never been done before. The streak started on May 19 when Long hit a home run in a victory against the Cubs. A week after his home run against the Cubs, he set a major league record against the Phillies with a home run in his seventh consecutive game. After a Sunday rainout, Long faced the Dodgers' Carl Erskine at Forbes Field and extended his home run record to eight consecutive games. Plagued by injuries after his record-setting performance, he struggled the rest of the season, though he did set a single-season Pirates record for a left-hand hitter with 27 home runs. The following year, the Pirates traded Long to the Chicago Cubs.

32,221 SEE LONG SET HR MARK

Bob Friend Stops Bums on a 2-hitter To Win 8ᵗʰ, 3–2

May 29, 1956
By Al Abrams
Pittsburgh Post-Gazette

Dale Long rewrote his amazing home run record and Bob Friend twirled a two-hitter last night at Forbes Field as the equally amazing Pirates bumped off the Brooklyn Dodgers, 3–2, before a delirious throng of 32,221.

The largest night game turnout since July 21, 1950, saw Long ram out his eighth home run in as many consecutive contests to crack his own mark of seven, which he set only last Saturday in Philadelphia.

He Homers in Fourth

The big first sacker's blow came in the fourth inning with none on base but it tied the score 2-all. It barely cleared the barrier in right center at a point approximately 380 feet from the plate.

No sooner had Long's bat connected with the ball than a roar came from the monster throng. The customers cheered the historic clout all the while Dale circled the bases and then did something never seen in the history of Forbes Field.

To a man, woman, and child, the 32,221 fans gave Long a standing ovation that lasted for several minutes, meanwhile holding up the game.

The modest Dale, all but mobbed by his teammates, acknowledged the greetings by going to the top step of the Pirate dugout and doffing his cap several times while the mob roared.

Oh Well, He Fanned Twice

This was Long's only hit of the game but it was enough to become historic. On three other trips to the plate, he struck out twice and bounced out to Pee Wee Reese who was playing second base in the exaggerated shift the Dodgers used every time Dale came to the plate.

Sharing equal billing with Long in the winning heroics was Friend who recorded his eighth triumph of the season against two defeats. It was Bob's

Pirate Dale Long hit a home run in eight consecutive games in 1956. (*Post-Gazette* archives)

sixth straight win at Forbes Field. He didn't allow a hit after the third inning when Gilliam singled to right.

Outside of an unusual streak of wildness, Friend mastered the hard-hitting Dodger lineup like he owned them. He walked six men, five of them coming as the first batters in an inning but outside of the first none of these proved harmful.

Snider Hits Homer

Jim Gilliam was the recipient of Friend's first gift and he romped home in front of Duke Snider when the latter blasted a ball over the right center field fence at a point between the Dreyfuss Monument and the iron gate. This was even longer than Long's terrific wallop last week.

The homer gave the Brooks a 2–0 lead behind the talented Carl Erskine but the Bucs chipped away to one run in the second. Long's homer tied it in the fourth, and the game-winning tally came in the fifth on Hank Foiles' triple and Bob Skinner's pitch single.

Overlooked in the general excitement was Dick Groat's sensational fielding at short and two remarkable one-handed catches by Duke Snider in center field.

The victory was the Pirates' fourth in a row, seventh in the last eight, and 11th in the last 15 to further cement their hold on third place in the standings.

20

Don Hennon Sets Pitt Record with 45 Points in a Double-Overtime Win against Duke

1957

In the same 1954–1955 season that Duquesne won the NIT, tiny Wampum, Pennsylvania, went 31–0 on its way to a WPIAL title. Its coach, L. Butler Hennon, appeared on the cover of *Life* magazine because of his unorthodox training methods, while his son, Don, set the all-time scoring record in the WPIAL. A 5'8" guard, Don Hennon accepted a scholarship to Pitt where he became an All-American in 1958 and 1959. His 24.2 points per game average is the best in Pitt's basketball history. In 1957, Hennon set Pitt's single-game record by scoring 45 points in a thrilling double-overtime victory against nationally ranked Duke. His 45 points remain the second most ever scored against a Duke team and is still the highest total ever scored by a Pitt player in a single game. The NBA drafted Hennon, but he decided to attend Pitt's medical school.

PITT'S HENNON LEADING NATION IN SCORING WITH 31.2 AVERAGE

December 23, 1957
By Myron Cope
Pittsburgh Post-Gazette

Don Hennon, who scored 45 points Saturday as he put on a two-hour television performance worthy of an Emmy Award, is leading the nation in scoring, unofficial figures showed last night.

Hennon, rewriting the Pitt record book in an 87–84 victory over Duke, raised his average from 27.8 points per game to 31.2 and now is three-tenths of a point ahead of 7-foot Wilt (The Stilt) Chamberlain of Kansas.

Chamberlain is averaging 30.9 and Oscar Robertson of Cincinnati is right behind with 30.8. On Saturday night Chamberlain was held to 19 points as his Kansas team beat California and Robertson was held, if that is the word, to 25 as his Cincinnati team beat Houston.

Does It In Overtime

Two overtime periods in which Hennon scored 11 points enabled him to pass up the two giants with whom he is battling for the national scoring title.

NCAA headquarters reported that complete returns from weekend games were not in yet, and therefore Hennon could not be officially ranked as the No. 1 scorer. However, barring the chance that some player brought off a spectacular performance unnoticed, *Post-Gazette* compilations show that the guy at the head of the pack is 5-foot-8 Don.

And so, Pitt's wagon is hitched to a star of the first order as the Panthers, like Duquesne, prepare to go social climbing this week, seeking national prestige in stiff holiday tournaments.

For coaches Dudey Moore and Bob Timmons, it is a nice spot to be in. Nobody expects the Dukes to win the Dixie Classic at Raleigh, North Carolina, and nobody expects Pitt to win the Holiday Festival in New York, but on the other hand, both teams have enough going for them to rate the role of dark horse.

Pitt's Don Hennon set the school's single-game scoring record with 45 points against Duke in December 1957. (*Post-Gazette* archives)

Both the Panthers and Dukes will plunge into the tournament swim Thursday afternoon. Pitt (4–1) goes against rebounding Temple (3–2) at Madison Square Garden while Duquesne (3–2) has an easier assignment against Wake Forest (2–5) at North Carolina State's 13,000-seat Reynolds Coliseum.

Duquesne's chances of survival, while better than Pitt's, may depend on the starting lineup that will be minus leading scorer 6-foot-6 Bob dePalma. This probably is not a serious handicap, however.

DePalma to Be Benched

Matthews is suffering from a pulled groin tendon but actually the injury is not considered severe enough to keep him benched if needed. DePalma incurred a badly bruised hand in last week's loss to Bowling Green. However, bruised hand or no bruised hand, he was in line to be benched because he has not been grabbing off as many rebounds as he did last season.

Moore plans to start 6-4 sophomore George Brown, a hot item against Bowling Green, and 6-6 sophomore Frank Grabowski, who, it is said, needs only a shot of confidence to perform adequately. At any given rate, the lineup changes give the Dukes additional height.

Should they get by Wake Forest, they will meet the winner of the Northwestern–North Carolina State game on Friday. Other teams in the affair, which runs Thursday through Saturday, include St. Louis, Seton Hall, North Carolina, and Duke.

The Pitt-Temple game offers New York fans the delight of watching two brilliant players. Hennon and Temple's 6-foot Guy Rodgers, choose their weapons.

A Pitt win would match the Panthers against the winner of the Seattle Connecticut game. The Holiday Festival, which will run Thursday, Saturday, and Monday, also includes Dayton, New York University, and Manhattan.

Hennon's 45-point television "Emmy" performance broke Ed Parlich's record of 40 and Ohio State star Robin Freeman's Field House record of 42.

21

Arnold Palmer Wins
First Masters

1958

The legend began when Deacon Palmer, the local professional and groundskeeper at the Oakmont Country Club, handed his young son, Arnold, a sawed-off golf club. Arnold Palmer became a child prodigy on the golf course and as a teenager won the Pennsylvania high school golfing championship twice before accepting a scholarship at Wake Forest. He turned professional in 1954 after winning the United States Amateur Championship. His Masters victory in 1958 was the first of seven major titles and catapulted him into national prominence. Famous for his late charges in tournaments, he developed a loyal following that became known as "Arnie's Army." Probably more than any other golfer, Palmer was responsible for the growing popularity of golf once television began to cover the sport. Jack Nicklaus, Palmer's chief rival on the links, won more majors, but Palmer, with his dynamic personality, was always the favorite of golfing fans and arguably the most beloved athlete in Western Pennsylvania sports history.

ARNIE PALMER WINS MASTERS BY ONE STROKE

His 284 Edges Ford, Hawkins

Rule on Imbedded Ball Gives Young Latrobe Golfer Victory

April 7, 1958
By Phil Gundelfinger
Pittsburgh Post-Gazette

AUGUSTA, GEORGIA—April 6—Arnold Palmer, a product of Western Pennsylvania fairways, carved a permanent niche in golf here today by winning the 22nd annual Masters tournament from a strong field with a 72-hole total of 284, four under par, at the sun-kissed and windswept Augusta National course.

The Latrobe touring pro shot a final 73, one over par, to hold off the final charge of defending champion Doug Ford of Mahopac, New York, and Fred Hawkins of El Paso, Texas, by one shot each.

Ford had a final 70 and Hawkins a 71 to deadlock for second place with 285.

Three-Putt Final

Palmer three-putted the final green from 65 feet to give Ford and Hawkins, playing together, chances to tie him if they could make birdies on the last green.

But Fred missed a 14-footer and then Ford missed a 10-footer and the tournament had its youngest champion since Bryon Nelson, then 24, won it in 1937. Arnie was 28 on last September 10.

The triumph was the biggest financial haul in Palmer's 3½-year pro career. With the 125 percent boost in the total purse, Arnie won $11,250 for first place. His biggest previous check was $7,500 for a victory in the Houston Open in February 1957.

Has Won $19,833.33

This also boosts Palmer into the top money-winning position for 1958.

Previous to the Masters he had won $8,633.33 for fourth place and hence he now has $19,833.33.

Ford and Hawkins won $4,500 each.

In the tie for fourth position at 286 were Ken Venturi of San Francisco and Stan Leonard of Vancouver, British Columbia. Venturi, the first and second round leader, had a final round of 72. Leonard, a six-time Canadian PGA champion; posted a 71. Each won $1,968.75.

Art Wall, Jr., of Pocono Manor, Pennsylvania, and Cary Middlecoff of Hollywood, Florida, tied for sixth with 287 and won $1,518.75 each. Wall has a final 74 and Middlecoff a 75.

Low Amateur was Billy Joe Patton, 35-year-old Morganton, North Carolina, lumberman, who shot a 74 today.

In a four-way deadlock at 289 and winning $1,265.63 each were: Claude Harmon, Mamaroneck, New York (70); Billy Maxwell, Odessa, Texas (76); Al Mengert, Westfield, New Jersey (74); and Jay Hebert, Sanford, Florida (71).

Snead Blows Up

Twelfth-place money of $1,125 went to Sam Snead of White Sulphur Spring, West Virginia, who blew to a final 79 for 290. He had been tied with Palmer for the 54-hole lead at 211.

Ben Hogan, Mike Souchak, and Jimmy Demaret finished in a tie for 13th with 291s. Each received $1,050.

An almost nerveless player, Arnie, nevertheless, came up to this tourney fatigued.

He had to engage in a playoff for the Azalea Open at Willmington, North Carolina, last Monday, and then came right over here. He played 18 holes Tuesday, played nine and then practiced on Wednesday.

Then "when I arose on Thursday I felt good and strong and thought I might do well," he said.

At the start he had one thing in mind: he would try to play as former champions had; to gamble at certain points and to be conservative at others.

Gets Eagle on 13th

A feature of his final round was an eagle three at the 475-yard 13th hole. He had a good drive and then knocked a choke No. 3 wood to 15 feet from the can and holed the putt.

It came after he had incurred a mired ball at the 155-yard 12th hole and had to play a provisional ball. He could have been given a five there but the official ruling, not given to Palmer until he was on the No. 15 fairway, was that he had scored a par three. The area had previously been declared wet and a free lift allowed.

Palmer was paired with Venturi, the coast phenom, in the final round and they carried a large section of the 20,000 fans around with them.

Arnie holed a fine 12-footer from the apron for a par at No. 1 to keep from losing more than one stroke there to Ken, who canned a 30-footer for a bird.

Venturi picked up another one at the fourth with an eight-footer for a deuce and he got even with Palmer at the next one when Arnie three-putted. Then Palmer got it back as Ken three-putted the next one and went two ahead with a nine-foot bird putt at No. 8, after which Venturi missed from five feet for his bird.

Ken Through at 16th

Venturi three-putted number 14 and 16 and that killed him off. Middlecoff caved in with a 38 going out and a bogey on No. 14; Wall was dead after bogeys at No. 12 and 13. A 38 going out crumpled Maxwell.

Wininger folded spectacularly with a nine on the 445-yard 11th hole. His drive landed in a tractor mark, and after he was refused a casual water lift, he hit one into the creek, the next one into a trap, and finally three-putted.

Arnie termed his victory "the greatest of my career."

He said his expectant wife, Winnie, who is here, was "very happy once we were sure I had won." They have one daughter now.

Started in WPIAL

The career started in 1943 with play in the WPIAL tourney and extended through two high school titles, five West Penn amateurs, an Ohio amateur, a Cleveland amateur, a Southern Intercollegiate, and finally, the United States Amateur in 1954. He played No. 1 at Wake Forest College.

He won the Canadian Open in 1955, the Panama and Columbian opens in 1956; four pro tour events in 1957, and one this year—the St. Petersburg Open two weeks ago.

His putting throughout the tourney was superb. This former Achilles' heel in his game was so perfected that he three-putted only four greens in the 72 holes.

He has arrived.

22

Harvey Haddix's Perfect No-Hitter for 13 Innings against the Braves

1959

Harvey Haddix was an unlikely candidate to pitch what has been called "the greatest game in baseball history." As a rookie with the Cardinals in 1953, he was a 20-game winner and won 18 games the following year. But, after being struck on the knee by a line drive, he struggled on the mound and moved from team to team until the Reds traded him in 1959, with Smoky Burgess and Don Hoak, to the Pirates for hometown hero Frank Thomas. On May 26, 1959, at Milwaukee County Stadium, Haddix faced a Braves team that included future Hall of Famers Eddie Mathews and Hank Aaron and pitched twelve perfect innings before losing 1–0 in the 13th inning. A little more than a year later, Haddix became the winning pitcher in the seventh and deciding game of the 1960 World Series.

HADDIX RETIRES 36, LOSES, 2-0

High Slider Cost Me Game, Says Harvey

That Was Pitch Adcock Hit in the 13th; Haddix Unaware He Had Perfect Game

May 27, 1959
By Jack Hernon
Pittsburgh Post-Gazette

MILWAUKEE—May 26—The little southpaw sat in front of his locker in the Pirate clubhouse. He was surrounded by the inquisitive members of the press.

"Joe hit a high slider," Harvey Haddix said. He made this statement while many other Bucs sat around the clubhouse bewildered. How could a fellow pitch so well and lose?

"It was a damn shame," Danny Murtaugh remarked. The manager had walked out of the dugout when the game ended on Adock's over-the-fence double and shook the hand of Haddix, patting him on the back for a fine job.

Small consolation though.

"I thought I had fine control all night," Harvey said. "I made a few bad pitches. The one to Adcock has to go down as a bad pitch.

"There were a few others, I don't remember when or what they were.

"Sure I knew I had the no-hitter. Now and then I would look at the scoreboard to see what the count was on a hitter. I had to see that zero back of the Braves.

"I didn't know about the perfect game though. I thought that maybe back there in the early innings I might have walked a man.

Just Another Loss

"How did I feel about it? It's just another loss and that's not good for myself or the club.

"I just wanted to keep them from scoring, that's all I was interested in. But we just didn't get that run I needed.

"I was pitching Adcock about the same way all night and that last time I

Pirates Harvey Haddix (left) and Smokey Burgess pore over the day's news in 1959.
(*Post-Gazette* archives)

didn't get away with it. The slider was high and we lost."

Fred Haney, in the Brave clubhouse, said. "That's the greatest game I've ever seen pitched."

Smoky Burgess thought that umpire Vinnie Smith had missed a pitch on Mantilla in the 13th inning. "We had him struck out," Smoky stated.

Haddix said he had tired in the last few innings. He turned to one reporter and said:

"You could see it, couldn't you? They were getting the ball up in the air a little more than I wanted them to.

Harvey Haddix on the mound, May 26, 1959, during what is considered by some to be the greatest game ever pitched. (*Post-Gazette* archives)

"I came close once before to a no-hitter. That was with the Cardinals in 1954. I went into the ninth and had one out to go against the Phils when Richie Ashburn got a hit. And I think Gran Hamner got another but I won that game."

Virdon Sent Deep

The tired feeling that Haddix spoke of arrived in the 10th when pinch hitter Del Rice and Ed Mathews both sent Bill Virdon to the edge of the cinder patch for fly balls. And in the 11th Del Crandall hit probably the hardest ball of the game, a line drive right at Virdon in center.

But for nine innings, only a line drive by Johnny Logan in the third was hard hit. It was a high drive which Dick Schofield grabbed above his head.

And so history in pitching was written, but on a sorry note for the 155-pound, 33-year-old Pirate lefthander.

23

Pirates World Series Victory over the New York Yankees

1960

It was the World Series that made Mickey Mantle cry and brought tears of joy to Pittsburgh fans, who turned the Downtown area into a Mardi Gras frenzy. After the dark days of the 1950s, the Pirates produced a miracle season of late-inning victories in 1960 and won the franchise's first National League pennant since 1927. In the World Series, they would once again face a powerful New York Yankees club, as they had when they were swept in 1927. In a seesaw series of lopsided Yankee wins and closely fought Pirates victories, baseball's world championship was finally decided in a wild, unpredictable seventh and deciding game. In the bottom of the ninth, with the score tied 9–9, Bill Mazeroski led off the inning and with one swing of the bat produced the most dramatic moment in Pittsburgh sports history.

WE HAD 'EM ALL THE WAY: BUCS ARE THE CHAMPS

Maz's Homer in the 9ᵗʰ Wins, 10–9

Pirates Come From Behind To Cop Series

Five-Run Rally in 8ᵗʰ Inning Breaks Yankee Lead as Smith Brings in 3 Runs with 4-Bagger

October 14, 1960
By Jack Hernon
Pittsburgh Post-Gazette

THE HOME OF THE WORLD CHAMPS—October 13—Bill Mazeroski sailed a homer out of Forbes Field on the second pitch in the ninth inning and the Pirates were champions of the world of baseball.

They came from behind with a roaring five runs in the eighth when Hal Smith—an old Yankee—hit a three-run homer and then won in the ninth, 10–9, over Casey Stengel's crowd of bruisers.

Mazeroski, who must be the greatest .270 hitter in baseball—he is today, that's for certain—went sailing around the bases waving his hat in one hand and pandemonium broke loose among the 36,683 patrons.

Ralph Terry, the 22-year-old righty of the Yanks, was the loser and Harvey Haddix, who put the Bucs in front three to two by winning the fifth game in Yankee Stadium, now has two World Series pitching victories.

The Yankees had roughed up Vern Law and Roy Face and Bob Friend to take a 7–5 lead, but Dan Murtaugh's brash Buccos wouldn't quit.

And who will say they backed into Pittsburgh first world title since 1925?

It was the third time now that the Pirates have been baseball's kingpins. And it was a sight to see them do it the Yankee way, after being tagged as a club that "hits one over this way and one over that way," by Casey.

Three Homers

Today they hit three home runs. Rocky Nelson, who could be wearing the

Danny Murtaugh congratulates Bill Mazeroski after the Pirates' 1960 World Series victory over the Yankees. (Paul Slantis/*Post-Gazette*)

goat's horns this morning, socked one in the first inning then along came the Smith boy in the eighth and the Mazeroski kid in the ninth.

Two of Stengel's maulers had hit home runs, raising their series total to 10, and they set all kinds of records, individual and otherwise. But then what the hell, let them have them, the Pirates have what they came out to get 10 days ago.

Five of the New York pitchers got into the ball game as the Pirates collected 11 hits and made them all big ones too as they left only one runner on base during the afternoon of Pittsburgh success.

Yogi Berra, the record-breaking catcher and left fielder for the New Yorkers, had sent the American League champs sailing into a lead in the sixth inning, shortly after the Bullpen Baron had replaced the Deacon.

He hit a three-run homer into the upper deck of the right field stands and the golden arm of the Pirate bullpen stood at a chance of becoming the losing pitcher.

But his guitar-playing partner, Smitty, erased those chances with his three-run belt off Jim Coates in the Buc eighth, a 430 footer.

And with that the Baron had an opportunity to become the winner, but Bob Friend couldn't get either of the first two Yanks out in the ninth and Haddix had to get called.

And he almost—but not quite—pitched the victory right then and there. A run had scored when Mickey Mantle singled and there was a runner on third.

Berra hit a hard grounder to first where Rocky scooped the ball and stepped on first. But Mantle scrambled back in on his belly to ruin the double play, which would have ended it right then and there.

But Rocky made the play backwards, instead of tagging Mantle first, and the tying run came home, but the Mazeroski boy took the Rock off the hook and gave Harvey the victory.

The one that Billy the Kid will remember the rest of his life didn't go as far as Smitty's into the Schenley Park trees, but those 420 feet or so it covered will do until another year.

Little Shantz, who again was brilliant in relief, until he sagged in the eighth, after pitching one-hit ball for five innings, saw his shortstop injured by a hot grounder off Bill Virdon's bat.

Kubek Injured

Gino Cimoli had looped a single to right, hitting for the Baron, when Virdon hit to short. The ball took a bad hop and hit Tony Kubek in the larynx for a base hit. The shortstop was taken from the game and to Eye and Ear Hospital by Dr. Henry Sherman for examination as he was spitting up blood.

Then came a ringing single to left by Dick Groat to score Gino and Coates was called on to pitch.

The celebration starts as Bill Mazeroski approaches home plate, about to score the winning run in the 1960 World Series. (James G. Klingensmith/*Post-Gazette*)

Bob Skinner, returning to the lineup for the first time since being injured in game one, sacrificed. But after Rocky flied to right, Bob Clemente beat out a slow bounder to Skowron as Virdon scored. Then the count on Smitty went to two-two and whack. He hit the ball and Coates threw his glove up in the air, as Smitty joyfully ran around the bases for a three-run homer.

But the Yankees came roaring back to tie in their part of the ninth. Bobby Richardson and Dale Long—an old Bucco— singled against Friend and that brought the call for Haddix.

Roger Maris lifted a foul to Smitty back of the plate but Mantle singled to right scoring Richardson and putting Long at third. Gil McDougald ran from there for Dale and scored the run which made it 9–9 when Rocky failed to make the double play backwards.

Prior to the wild finish to the most exciting game in the Series, the Pirates had run up a lead of four for the Deacon in two innings.

Turley, who had won 16–3 over the Pirates in the second game, was clipped for a quick deuce in the first. He had two out when he walked Skinner and Rocky sent a two-one pitch over the right-field screen and the champs were on the way, although later it looked like a black afternoon for them.

In the next inning Turley was rapped for a single by Smoky Burgess and that brought on Bill Stafford.

He walked Don Hoak on four pitches. Maz—OUR HERO—was up to sacrifice but instead beat out his bunt for a full house.

Then Law bounced back to the mound for a home-first base double play. Bill Virdon gave the Pirates two with a single into center. For two and two-thirds innings the Deacon was perfect. Hector Lopez ended this with a pinch-single to left for Stafford.

And in the fourth there was another hit and in the fifth Skowron hit into the right field stands for his second homer of the set and sixth one of the World Series.

The next round was fatal as the Yanks went ahead, 5–4.

Richardson looped a single to center and Kubek walked. On came the Baron in this spot to retire Maris on a foul to Hoak. But Mantle singled to center scoring a run and Yogi sent Pirate hopes and the fans into the doldrums with a homer upstairs in right field, his 11th one of the fall.

And in the eighth they scored two more and it appeared that was going to be the windup of the Pirates for the season.

The Baron retired the first pair but walked Berra. Skowron hit a high bounder to Hoak and his throw wasn't fast enough to get Yogi at second base.

John Blanchard then looped a base hit to right scoring Berra. Clete Boyer doubled to left scoring Skowron before Shantz went out.

But our gang wasn't through and then went roaring on to the title with the five runs in the eighth and the one-run ninth by the Mazeroski boy.

And they hailed the new champions of baseball after that sock ended the game with the Pirates in front 10–9.

24

Led by MVP Connie Hawkins, Pipers Win ABA Championship

1968

There were the ill-fated and short-lived Pittsburgh Ironmen of the BAA in 1946 and the Pittsburgh Rens of the ABL in 1961, but it would take a team of misfits, outcasts, and outlaws playing with a red, white, and blue basketball to bring a major pro basketball championship to Pittsburgh in 1968. Led by MVP Connie Hawkins, who was banned by the NCAA and NBA for his alleged association with a gambling scandal, the Pittsburgh Pipers, in the first year of the ABA, overcame a 3–2 deficit against the New Orleans Buccaneers and won the seventh and deciding game at the Civic Arena. The Pipers, despite their success, became a one-season wonder. Because of poor attendance, they moved to Minnesota for the following season. Connie Hawkins, after a court decision exonerated him, went on to play and star in seven seasons in the NBA with the Suns, Lakers, and Hawks.

CLINCH ABA TITLE BEFORE 11,457

Pipers Plan to Go Again

May 6, 1968
By Jimmy Miller
Pittsburgh Post-Gazette

They no sooner ended one season and imbibed in a little spirited libation to celebrate winning everything to be won than the Pipers started plotting for another go in the American Basketball Association.

Gabe Rubin, executive director, and Vince Cazzetta, excellent coach of the excellent club, are in Minneapolis attending important meetings of the ABA at which they drafted 15 players and put in dire requests for certain dates in the schedule next season.

While he has regained a little of the optimism that got him into pro venture, Rubin still is willing to entertain any offer for the club that could get him off the hook, which according to reports, is baited with a loss of several hundred thousand.

It's no secret that Rubin as late as Friday was ready to shuck it all. But he did break into smiles about the rabid crowd of 11,457 that turned out for last Saturday night's ulcer-producing 122–113 championship victory over the New Orleans Buccaneers at the Civic Arena.

When the drove of young fans carried a number of the Pipers off the court, Rubin said he had new feelings, saying, "This crowd is something else. May be the fans finally have adopted us."

Prior to the big turnout, Rubin was in deep despair over the apathy of the fans toward an exciting team that kept providing itself week after week. The average turnout for the season was about 3,200 per game.

While the brass is at the confabs, the Piper players have made plans for sundry ways to spend the off-season. After they guzzled some champagne and beer in the dressing room and gave beer baths to each other and a shower to Alex Medich, their trainer, the happy bunch started to disband.

Connie Hawkins, praised by every coach in the ABA as one of the greatest

Pittsburgh Pipers teammates (from left) Chico Vaughn, Art Heyman, Connie Hawkins, and Charley Williams. (*Post-Gazette* archives)

players in the game today, is going to continue treatments for his right knee, which has a torn medial tendon. After the hurt has healed, Connie will probably take that European tour with the Globetrotters.

Charley Williams, the classy little backcourter who, along with Hawkins was voted to the all-league team, has departed for his home in Seattle; Jimmy Jarvis, the alternate guard, will have X-rays taken of the calcium deposit on his right thigh today, which may lead to early surgery. He will spend the summer here.

Leroy Wright leaves today for St. Albans, Queens, and his job with the Tuck Tape Co.; Art Heyman, the charging upfront vet, is back in New York and will operate his restaurant; Tom Washington, the other forward is going back to Philadelphia next Saturday and will take exercises to help strengthen his left wrist fractured in a pre-season game.

Another hospital case is Guard Arvesta Kelly. He will undergo the knife at West Penn Hospital next week to correct a knee condition.

Craig Dill, a pivot, left for his home in Saginaw, Michigan; Willie Porter takes off for Berkeley, California, tomorrow; Rich Parks heads for St. Louis on Wednesday and Steve Vacendak is going to North Carolina before arriving home in Scranton in time for his sister's wedding on May 25.

Of course, before they all went their merry ways, the small subject of what to do with $39,800 won in playoff pots was thoroughly discussed. How the split was made was never known.

Cazzetta, who incidentally has to be named coach of the year if the voting is not of the old Philadelphia variety, was lavish in his praise of the club.

"This was a fighting club all year," said Cazzetta. "And it deserved to win as it did. We had to play another standout game Saturday night in order to beat New Orleans, a well-coached and strong club.

"You can't say enough nice things about Hawkins, who I judge the best in pro ball; Williams, who is one of the top guards, will become better; Washington, who has given us some good defensive work; Heyman, whose spirit and drive were hard to match; Vaughn, who plays both ways with finesse; and Jarvis, who has been more than an able sub man in the backcourt."

Babe McCarthy, coach of the Bucs, also praised the Pipers and Cazzetta but was a bit irked over the fact that one official—Joe Belmont—worked four of the seven playoff games between the clubs.

"I'm not critical of the work of the officials but I didn't feel that one man should have worked four games. Other officials did a fine job all season and they did not get a chance at working our series. I don't know if the Pipers had a choice of officials or not but I know we did not."

Bill Hosket, the 6–10 pivot of Ohio State who is being wooed by the Pipers and the New York Knicks of the NBA, saw the title game and was impressed with the Pipers' play and the enthusiasm of the young fans.

25

Pirates World Series Victory over the Baltimore Orioles

1971

On June 28, 1970, the Pirates played their last game at Forbes Field. Appropriately, Bill Mazeroski, the hero of the 1960 World Series, fielded the last out in a victory against the Chicago Cubs. A little more than a year later, the Pirates, playing in Three Rivers Stadium, won the Eastern Division title, defeated Willie Mays and the San Francisco Giants in the National League Playoffs, and met Brooks Robinson and the Baltimore Orioles in the 1971 World Series. The Pirates won the World Series in good part because of the outstanding pitching of Steve Blass and a clutch relief appearance by 21-year-old rookie Bruce Kison, but the 1971 World Series will always be remembered as the showcase for Roberto Clemente. The Great One fielded brilliantly, batted .414, homered in the seventh and deciding game, won by the Pirates 2–1, and was selected overwhelmingly for the MVP Award.

WE'RE THE CHAMPS

Blass, Clemente Stop Orioles, 2–1

Roberto Slaps Homer, Steve 4-Hits Birds

October 18, 1971
By Charley Feeney
Pittsburgh Post-Gazette

BALTIMORE—The drama-packed World Series is over but the memories—sweet memories—linger on.

The Pirates became world champions here yesterday in a tension-packed thriller against the Orioles who were beaten 2–1 by Steve Blass and Roberto Clemente in the seventh game of this 68th World Series.

Most of the 44,174 fans at Memorial Stadium came to see the Birds bury the Buccos. The Bucs, underrated but not overmatched, outfought the American League champions.

They outfought them because Clemente, 37 years young, belted a home run off loser Mike Cuellar in the fourth inning.

They outfought them because Jose Pagan, a clutch sub, delivered a scoring double in the eighth inning.

Blass, magnificent under Series pressure, held the Big Bird sluggers to four hits.

Blass challenged the Orioles, who a week ago seemed on their way to sweep when they won the first two games here. But Blass, with a three-hitter, turned the series around on Tuesday, then the Bucs kept coming off the floor and when Jackie Hernandez threw out Merv Rettenmund at 4:10 pm yesterday, the Bucs became world champions.

As Bob Robertson clinched the ball, Blass leaped in the air. Jackie Hernandez, his hands flying in all directions, raced to Blass. Robby got there first.

The Pirate dugout emptied. The victory party was on.

It was 1960 all over again. It was Pittsburgh's fourth world championship. All of them were won in seven games.

Tradition.

It's beautiful.

The Pirates' (from left) Bob Moose, Willie Stargell, and Bob Robertson sing a happy tune after getting a dunking in the dressing room. (Edwin Morgan/*Post-Gazette*)

Blass made only one big mistake yesterday and it wasn't a pitch: He fielded Tom Shopay's bunt in the eighth inning and didn't realize he had an easy force at third base.

Instead, Blass made sure of the easy out at first. He threw out Shopay, but now the Orioles had runners on second and third.

Elrod Hendricks, who singled, was on third and Mark Belanger, who also singled, was on second base with the tying run.

The Baltimore fans, who saw their Birds beat the Bucs, 3–2, in the 10th inning Saturday, were howling now. They had an idea the Birds were going to break through.

Don Buford, Saturday's bat hero, was the hitter. He bounced to Robertson, who was playing deep. Hendricks scored as the second out was made. Now Belanger was on third base—90 feet away from a tie.

Dave Johnson, the Birds' second baseman, was the hitter.

The Buc scouting report called for Hernandez to play Johnson in the left-side hole. Beautiful scouting report.

Johnson hit directly to Hernandez, who threw him out.

It wasn't a tough play, but when there was a tough play in this World Series, Jackie Hernandez made it. Hernandez, who erred at times during the season, had an excellent series.

He started six games because Gene Alley's left knee was hurting.

Hernandez didn't hurt the Bucs. He may not be a great player, but in the Series pressure, he responded brilliantly.

Saturday's game had more thrills than yesterday's contest, but the seventh game was what made this so big.

Clemente, voted the outstanding player in the Series, showed the American Leaguers that he just might be the best player in baseball. He showed them in every game. He showed them yesterday in the fourth inning when he belted a home run over the fence in left-center.

It was a first-pitch homer and it was the Bucs' first against Cuellar. Blass made it stand up for seven tough innings, then the Pirates got their biggest run of the baseball season in the eighth.

Stargell, who batted .206 in the Series, opened the eighth with a sharp ground single, which Birds shortstop Belanger failed to catch in a backhand try.

Stargell, because of his anemic hitting in the first six games, was dropped to sixth in the batting order yesterday with Robertson taking his spot at cleanup.

Pagan, who followed Stargell, lined deep to center: Rettenmund, who was playing shallow, never had a chance to make the catch. He had a chance at a quick relay, but blew it when he couldn't get the ball out of his glove.

Stargell, a slow Buc, slowed down rounding second fearing Rettenmund might make the catch. When the ball dropped in front of his face, Stargell put his 225 pounds in high gear. He slid across the plate while Hendricks stood helplessly. Powell cut off Belanger's relay.

The Bucs were on top 2–0. In the Birds' eighth, it became 2–1, then Blass had to face the meat of the Baltimore order.

The first hitter in the ninth was Big Boog Powell who had a worse bat Series than Stargell. He was three-for-27. Blass went to 2–2 on him before he bounced to Dave Cash. One out.

Frank Robinson was the next hitter. Last Tuesday in Pittsburgh, Frank Robinson hit a home run off Blass. Yesterday, he swung at Blass' first pitch in the ninth and popped it to Hernandez. Two out.

Rettenmund took Blass' first pitch for a strike. He bounced the next serve up the middle. It may have been a base hit for some hitters, but Pirate scouting report on the Orioles was in action again.

Hernandez was playing behind second for the right-handed hitting Rettenmund. Hernandez made the grab and fired to Robertson.

Three out and the world championship belongs to Pittsburgh.

During the first six games, the Pirates wasted many scoring chances. They had few against Cuellar yesterday.

Manny Sanguillen opened the fifth with a single to center, but the next three hitters couldn't produce.

The Bucs didn't get another man on base until the eighth when Stargell and Pagan combined for a run.

They got two singles off reliever Pat Dobson with two out in the ninth. Dave McNally, relieved, and Stargell rolled to Johnson at second.

Blass ran into difficulty in the second when, with one out, he walked Brooks Robinson and Bob Robertson fumbled Hendricks' grounder. Blass got Belanger to bounce a DP ball to Dave Cash.

Hendricks doubled to right center with one out in the fifth, but Belanger and Cuellar couldn't produce.

The next time the Birds put men on base was in the eighth. They scared the daylights out of the Pittsburgh fans watching the game on television. They didn't scare Steve Blass. He didn't crack.

When it was over, Blass explained his mistake on Shopay's pitch bunt.

"I wanted to make sure of the out," Blass said. "With the crowd yelling I didn't hear Sangy yell third base."

Sanguillen and Blass held a brief conference after the play.

"I tell him," Sanguillen said, "that I'm not mad at him. I tell him to keep pitching like he was."

Blass kept pitching like he was and that's why the Pirates are world champions today.

26

Roberto Clemente's 3,000th Hit

1972

When Roberto Clemente doubled off the Mets' Jon Matlack for his 3,000th hit, he joined an exclusive baseball club that included Honus Wagner and Paul Waner. Unlike Wagner and Waner, however, Clemente's hits were all made while he was in a Pirates uniform. At the age of 38, Clemente was in the twilight of his career, but no one could anticipate that his 3,000th hit would be the last of his regular-season career. In 1972, the Pirates were on their way to the National League playoffs after winning the Eastern Division, but their hopes of defending their World Series title ended with a heartbreaking loss to the Reds on a wild pitch. On December 31, heartbreak turned to tragedy when Clemente lost his life in a plane crash while trying to help the victims of an earthquake in Managua, Nicaragua.

FOR CLEMENTE AFTER 3,000, SATURDAY CHEERS LINGER

October 2, 1972
By Charley Feeney
Pittsburgh Post-Gazette

It was 3,000-hit day—plus one.

Roberto Clemente yesterday was given a trophy by some friends who came up from Puerto Rico to see him rap out hit No. 3,000 Saturday.

Yesterday, Clemente's friends honored him in pregame ceremonies. He did not play. The 30,031 prize-day fans at Three Rivers Stadium gave him a standing ovation before the game.

Later, when he warmed up Bob Miller between innings, Clemente was given a mild hand from the crowd. The cheers of Saturday were still with him yesterday.

"I felt kind of bashful when the fans cheered," Clemente said. "I'm a very quiet, shy person although you writers might not believe it because I shout sometimes."

There was no shouting yesterday. Clemente says he is tired. He will rest until the playoffs begin against the Reds on Saturday.

Clemente seemed to want to talk more about the fans than his achievement.

"We are here," he said, "for the purpose to win for the fans. That is who we work for. Not for Joe Brown. He does not pay our salary. The fans pay our salary."

If that is so, the Pittsburgh fans are paying Roberto Clemente more than $125,000 a year. The fans do not complain about his salary and neither do the Pirate owners who shell out the dough.

Clemente, 38 and in his 18th season, talked about old times and he talked about present-day players.

But somehow he couldn't forget the fans.

"After we won the World Series in 1960, I was criticized because I didn't stay around the clubhouse to celebrate," he said. "You know where I went. I went to Schenley Park to celebrate with the fans. We hugged each other. I felt good being with them."

When Clemente lined Jon Matlack's pitch into left-center field for a double Saturday, he became the 11th player in history to reach 3,000 hits.

One of the elite members of the 3,000-hit club was sitting in the Mets' dugout.

When the fifth inning ended, Mays left the Mets' dugout and went to the Pirate dugout where he shook hands with Clemente.

Later Clemente said: "Willie Mays is the greatest ball player I've ever seen. I never saw Joe DiMaggio play, but if Joe DiMaggio was better than Willie Mays he belongs in heaven."

Roberto Clemente acknowledges the cheers from the Pittsburgh crowd after getting his 3000th hit. (Morris Berman/*Post-Gazette*)

27

First Steelers Playoff Victory and the Immaculate Reception

1972

With the brash Bobby Layne throwing touchdown passes, the Same Old Steelers became entertaining in the early 1960s, but by the end of the decade they'd returned to their old losing ways. In 1969, they hired a bright young assistant coach from the Baltimore Colts, but, in Chuck Noll's first season with the team, the Steelers, at 1–13, finished with the worst record in pro football. With the No. 1 pick in the draft, the Steelers selected Terry Bradshaw.

Rebuilding the team through the draft, the Steelers finally won a division championship, their first title in franchise history, and met the Oakland Raiders in the playoffs at Three Rivers Stadium. With his team trailing by one point and only seconds left in the game, Franco Harris gave long-suffering Steelers fans the most memorable moment in Steelers history with his "immaculate reception."

LAST-MINUTE WIN DRIVES CROWD WILD

Santa Finds Steeler Fans Early

December 25, 1972
By Alvin Rosensweet
Pittsburgh Post-Gazette

On this Christmas Day—a Noel for Noll—there are Steeler fans who probably awakened early and repeated over and over to themselves:

"There is a Santa Claus."

They will believe in Santa Claus from now on and they will believe in mirages and illusion and the ethereal things of life that are not supposed to be true but somehow are.

Because if the Steelers won over the Oakland Raiders 13–7 Saturday—and they did—it is possible to believe in anything, including an ultimate victory in the Super Bowl.

There is something about pro football that generates an almost animalistic enthusiasm in otherwise peace-loving people and on Saturday between the hours of 1 and 4 PM, under a grey sky on a warm late-December afternoon, this intensity of the spirit emerged full-blown.

There are 60 minutes in a football game but this one first came down to a minute and 13 seconds when Oakland scored what obviously was the winning touchdown, and then it came down to the last 22 seconds when Franco Harris caught a bobbling forward pass and pulled, hauled, tugged, and strained down the sideline to somehow score the winning touchdown.

Instant replay may show that it never happened, that it was an illusory event that fooled players, fans, and officials alike. "Miracle" and "unbelievable" are clichés, inadequate adjectives to describe what really happened.

But when it happened, and perhaps it did, the stadium exploded into a standing, screaming, flag-waving, banner-waving mass of humanity,

Steeler players who might be pardoned for being blasé jumped and pounded on Harris like schoolboys. Thousands of fans leaped from their

Franco Harris is congratulated after the Immaculate Reception. (Morris Berman/ *Post-Gazette*)

seats onto the field, surrounding their heroes as men in another age might have paid tribute to their gladiators.

It was a wild scene as men with infants in arms, young girls, and thousands of boys and men of all ages ran over the field jumping and hugging one another. From somewhere a new flag was unfurled, "Franco—Run Paisano, Run," and from the upper stands a new banner proclaimed, "Goodbye, Oakland, Bring on Miami." The scoreboard read "Merry Christmas" and over a loudspeaker a voice boomed:

"We're No. 1."

Diagram for unlikely victory: a collision between Oakland's Jack Tatum and Frenchy Fuqua sent a Terry Bradshaw pass flying back toward Franco Harris, who gathered the deflection and ran to history. (Donald J. Stetzer/*Post-Gazette*)

Somehow, Christmas came early for all those organization that have sprung up without benefit of charter: Franco's Italian Army, Gerela's Gorillas, Joe Greene's Polish Armed Forces, Green Babushkas, Russell's Raiders, the Crunch Bunch Dee-Fense, Ham's Hussars, Dwight's Whites, Rowser's Railroad, Iron Man Mansfield, Count Fuqua's Foreign Legion.

Their banners hung from upper tiers and along the sidelines like those held aloft to inspire an army's brigades into the fray.

But for most of the first half it was somewhat of a subdued crowd, standing and applauding, and granting most of its plaudits to the defense. Rarely, during those first two periods that ended without a score, did the Steeler fans have an opportunity to chant "Go, Go, Go" in behalf of the offense.

But there was something to cheer about in the third period as Roy Gerela, whose gifted toes are as talented as those of a Nureyev, kicked the first of two field goals. Up in Section 524 Steve Pavicic, a crippled man from Baldwin Borough, could screw up a smile and state unequivocally, "This is the happiest day of my life."

There were 3 minutes and 50 seconds to go and Gerela kicked another field goal and it was 6 to 0 for the Steelers and bands were playing and people were screaming and a sign announcing "No. 1 Super Steelers" went up and there was no way to lose the game or was there?

Gerela was toasting his gifted right foot in an instant warmer on the sidelines when Ken Stabler, who had come in at quarterback to light a fire under the Raiders, ran his left end for a touchdown on a play that was as improbable as Franco Harris' a few minutes later.

Suddenly it was 7 to 6, Oakland, and a crowd of 50,350 that had been jubilant a moment before was now depressed. There was no way for the Steelers to win and then with 22 seconds to go and on fourth down the Steelers called upon the powers of the occult and a touchdown was scored.

Outside the Stadium Mary Ann Katsur of Oakland—Pittsburgh's Oakland—wore a big "Oakland Raiders" button and waited for her brother, aging George Blanda, the Raiders' third-string quarterback and placekicker.

"They should have put the old-timer in," she said of her brother, but Oakland hadn't and Lamonica and Stabler and the rest of the Raiders, being only mortals, could not defeat a team of magicians.

For the Steelers, there is only one problem:

What can they possibly do for an encore?

28

Pitt Defeats Furman, Moves on to NCAA Elite Eight

1974

Once the eccentric Doc Carlson began coaching basketball at Pitt, the program took on national prominence. Though there were no championship tournaments at the time, Pitt teams, led by Charley Hyatt, were twice declared national champions in the late 1920s. In 1941, Pitt played in an NCAA final, but there were only eight teams competing in the tournament, which was only in its third year. When Bob Timmons replaced Carlson in 1953, his teams, during the Don Hennon years, played in two NCAA tournaments and appeared again in 1963. Westminster's coach Buzz Ridl replaced Timmons in 1968 and continued Pitt's winning tradition. In the 1973–1974 season. Pitt, led by Braddock native and All-American Billy Knight, went 25–4 and advanced to the NCAA's Elite Eight with victories over St. Joseph and Furman. Pitt lost its next game to the eventual tournament champion, North Carolina State, in a game played in North Carolina.

PITT BLOSSOMS OUT AGAINST FURMAN, 81-78

March 15, 1974
By Marino Parascenzo
Pittsburgh Post-Gazette

RALEIGH, NORTH CAROLINA—There was concern that a creep of Canadian air would snuff out the peach blossoms and the like here, but for the Pitt Panthers, it was a time of rebirth and flowering.

Billy Knight found his lost confidence, Kirk Bruce discovered that shooting can be fun as well as profitable, and the devilish Pitt defense found Furman's towering Paladins, and chilled them out for an 81–78 victory in the NCAA basketball Eastern Regional last night.

Fessor (Moose) Leonard, a spindly 7–1, and Clyde Mayes, a moose-like 6–9, might still be hunting their way out of difficulty but the floor had to be turned over to North Carolina State and Providence, who met in the second game of the doubleheader. Pitt will meet North Carolina State, a 92–78 winner in the windup, for the Eastern title tomorrow afternoon.

It will be strange country. Four previous Pitt teams have gone into the NCAA tourney, but none got as far as the Eastern final.

Coach Buzz Ridl, whose expression changes are about as noticeable as those at Rushmore, was a clearly pleased man. He had found his lost sheep. The whiz, the clock, and the whir were back after several weeks of absence.

Knight broke out of his slump like Mt. Etna disturbing the peace, hitting 12 of 20 shots and 10 of 11 free throws for a game-high 34 points. He also had seven rebounds, just one under Mayes tops of eight.

Bruce, who has been a reluctant shooter, went 6-for-9, and steady Lew Hill was 6-for-13. But that's box office stuff. It was Pitt without the ball that told the story.

Ridl's problem was clear—keep the ball from the big men inside. So was the solution, then, get on the guards like a case of rash.

It was blossom time, then, for Furman's Bruce Grimm, a freshman guard. While Mayes got only 11 points and Leonard 17, nether figure representing what should have been their true worth against the shorter Panthers, Grimm cut loose from outside and got 27.

He in fact kept Furman in the game and Pitt finally took control after he drew his fourth personal and went to a protective rest with 7:20 in the game.

He never did foul out, but it was after he came back, at 4:54, that Pitt started to wrap it up.

Bill hit a short jumper for a 74–72 edge, and while Knight was shooting a pair of free throws, Ridl called for his first timeout of the game at 3:04. It was no surprise that a stall was to follow, and when Furman decided to try a full-court press, it misfired and cost the slender Leonard his fifth foul at 1:49.

The "old" Pitt hung on in the opening minutes, when Furman moved out to leads of as much as six points.

"Then I switched our offense," Ridl said. "We went from our 1–3–1 offense to a box-and-one offense."

Functionally, this freed Pitt's superior speed against Furman's height and man-to-man defense (that was really Leonard and Mayes playing a kind of two-deep zone). Loose now, Pitt began hitting.

"No," Furman Coach Joe Leonard said, his purple suit burning out optic nerves all over the interview room, "we never considered going into a zone. We knew Pitt had trouble with the zone, but the man is what we do best. If we'd gone zone, I'm afraid all we'd have done is surprise ourselves."

Williams also credited the Pitt defense for upsetting his team, but he blamed the tension of a tourney appearance more.

Whatever it was, Furman, after getting up by six early, began to crack under the pressure—steps here, bad pass there, steal and block. The Paladins committed 25 turnovers, and it was the free throw line that kept them alive in the first half.

Pitt had 18 goals to Furman's 12, but Furman went 10-for-13 in free throws to Pitt's 2-for-2, and Pitt held a 38–34 halftime lead.

It didn't last. The teams returned to the seesaw, and Furman got up by as much as six again when Leonard took a high lob pass for an easy score at 11:58. And what could Pitt do against that kind of play? Nothing. But Pitt didn't have to. For some reason, Furman had not used it before and did not use it again.

Both Ridl and Williams conceded the greatness of North Carolina State and the power of Providence.

But Williams outdid Ridl in his surprise that Pitt has come this far. Ridl said he expected, say, an 18-victory season and probably the NIT. Williams has yet to believe Pitt has made it here.

"I was disappointed in our defense," he said. "We had trouble matching up with Penn."

29

Carol Semple Thompson Wins British Amateur Championship after Winning U.S. Open a Year Earlier

1974

Sewickley's Carol Semple Thompson was to woman's golf in the 1970s what Arnold Palmer was to men's golf in the late 1950s and 1960s. Like Palmer, Semple Thompson grew up in a golfing family. Her father, Bud Semple, was an accomplished golfer and became the president of the United States Golf Association from 1973–1974. Her mother, Phyllis Semple, was an outstanding amateur golfer. When a young Carol Semple won the Western Pennsylvania Women's Championship at the age of 16, she had to defeat her mother in match play on her way to her first golfing title. During her career, Semple Thompson won seven major USGA championships, including the US Amateur Open in 1973 and the British Amateur Open in 1974. In 2008, she joined fellow Western Pennsylvanian Arnold Palmer in the World Golf Hall of Fame.

ONLY CLUBS IN HER BAG OF TRICKS

Semple Captures British Am

June 17, 1974
By Jimmy Jordan
Pittsburgh Post-Gazette

Overseas reports to the contrary, Carol Semple does not play golf while in a daze, under hypnosis, nor in a trance.

Nor in any combination of the above.

Miss Semple has added the British Women's Amateur title to her US Women's Amateur crown and she insists she did so without any hocus-pocus or hexes influencing her choice of shots or her swing.

She defeated Angela Bonallack, 37-year-old wife of a former British Walker Cup captain, 2 & 1, on the Royal Porthcawl Golf Course in Wales Saturday to win the British crown.

Carol, 25, became the first American woman ever to win both the U.S. and British championships since 1948—before she was born. Louise Suggs was the last to win 'em both.

Miss Semple, reached by telephone at the home of a friend in London yesterday, still was excited by the victory—a "Grand Slam" of women's amateur golf, actually—but she also was a bit upset over some of the news service stories about the championship.

The stories indicated that a tape that she often plays before a match puts her into a state of hypnosis, which lasts through the day's play.

"That's not true," she told the *Post-Gazette*. "I do have a tape that I often play before I go to the golf course, but all it does is help my concentration. It does not put me in a trance or a hypnotic state, or anything like that.

"Actually, I don't see how I could hit a golf ball if I were in a trance."

Her combination for victory more likely is her ability to size up a shot properly, wonderful coordination in hitting the ball and confidence.

"I think I was in a daze when the match ended and I realized I had won this big tournament, but I know I wasn't in a daze while I was playing," the daughter of H.S. (Bud) Semple, president of the United States Golf Association said.

The Sewickley family is one of golf's most prominent. Carol's mother, Phyllis, has won innumerable titles. So have others in the family.

"I had won the Women's West Penn, the Pennsylvania State and others, all of them great, but nothing of national importance until I won the U.S. championship," Carol said. "And now this. I'm still excited about it."

Her father, reached at the U.S. Open at Mamaroneck, New York, said that he thought weather at Porthcawl would bother Carol, "but apparently it didn't."

Miss Semple had been playing well just before going to Wales. She shot a 68, two under men's par, at Allegheny Country Club despite being four over par on the last three holes.

Bobby Cruickshank, the veteran Scot who is still beating his age at 77,

Golfer Carol Semple Thompson won both the U.S. Women's Amateur and British Women's Amateur titles. (*Post-Gazette* archives)

Frank Smith and Chuck Scally, former Tri-State PGA and Open champ, are the teachers who helped build her championship game.

"Chucky Scally worked with me for about a week and a half before I came over here," she said.

She credited a fine bunker shot on the 17th of the final round as the "winner."

"It was 40 to 50 yards and stopped three feet from the pin. I was two up at the time. Mrs. Bonallack, after putting for a five, conceded me a half on the hole, and the 2 & 1 win," Carol explained. "Without that shot we would have gone to the 18th dormie and then anything could happen."

She plans to take part in a celebrity-type tournament at Youngstown in a few days, and then will hone her game for the Broodmoor Invitational at Colorado Springs, and the West Penn and State women's tournaments.

And she'll play them with a clear-thinking brain, muscular coordination, and golf clubs—not with hypnosis choosing her clubs and making the shots.

First Steelers AFC Championship

1974

After easily defeating O. J. Simpson and the Buffalo Bills, the Steelers advanced to the AFC Championship Game for the second time in three years. For the third consecutive playoff season, they faced the Oakland Raiders. After defeating the defending Super Bowl champion Miami Dolphins in a dramatic last-second victory, the Raiders believed they had already won the right to play in the Super Bowl. The Raiders had handily won last year's playoff game against the Steelers in Oakland, 33–14, but a year later, a healthier Steelers team with a Steel Curtain defense and a more confident Terry Bradshaw were ready for the Raiders. The defense held Oakland's running attack to 29 yards for the game, but the Steelers trailed 10–3 going into the fourth quarter. Sparked by critical interceptions from Jack Ham and J.T. Thomas and touchdowns by Franco Harris and Lynn Swann, the Steelers fought back to defeat the Raiders, 24–13, and earned the right to face the Minnesota Vikings in the Super Bowl.

STEELERS WIN, ON TO SUPER BOWL

Beat Raiders, 24–13; Vikings Next Jan. 12

December 30, 1974
By David Fink
Pittsburgh Post-Gazette

OAKLAND—Terry Bradshaw, a benchwarmer for the first half of the regular season, guided the Pittsburgh Steelers to a 23–13 upset victory over the Oakland Raiders in the American Football Conference Championship Game yesterday.

The triumph advanced the Steelers into the January 12 Super Bowl in New Orleans opposite National Conference king Minnesota, which beat Los Angeles 14–10 earlier in the day.

It was Pittsburgh's first AFC title. The trip to the Super Bowl will be a first for the team colorful Art Rooney founded 42 years ago.

Oakland's only first-half score followed a Lynn Swann fumble of a punt return at the Pittsburgh 41.

On third-and-5 from the Steelers' 23, Stabler's pass for Branch fell incomplete.

Later in the first quarter, the Steelers drove from the Oakland 47 to the Raiders' 3, but Roy Gerela shanked his 20-yard field goal try with 1:09 left.

The next time they owned the ball, the Steelers tied it. Starting from the midfield, they marched to the Raiders' six before Gerela booted a 23-yard field goal with 9:34 left in the half.

With the Steelers on the Raiders' 10-yard line, Wilson intercepted a Bradshaw-for-Stallworth pass and returned it to the Raider 35.

A 15-yard penalty against the Steelers moved the ball to midfield with Stabler passing for 27 to Biletnikoff and 12 to tight end Bob Moore, the Raiders reached the Pittsburgh 21. This time Jack Lambert blocked Blanda's 38-yard field goal, leaving the 3–3-deadlock intermission.

In the second half after a Walden punt rolled into the end zone, the Raiders went 80 yards in eight plays. Along the way, Stabler passed to Biletnikoff for eight and 10 and Branch for 20 and 38. That 38-yard pass, thrown over the usually dependable Mel Blount, was worth six points. Blanda's kick made it 10–3 with 5:05 left in the third quarter.

Pittsburgh retaliated immediately. With Harris gaining 16 yards, Bleier 35, and Bradshaw passing to Stallworth for a crucial 13, the Steelers drove 61 yards in nine plays. Harris got the final eight before Gerela's kick made it 10–10.

Ham's second interception and return to the Oakland nine set up the Steelers' go-ahead touchdown. A holding penalty against Oakland's Skip Thomas gave Pittsburgh the ball on the four.

Bleier gained nothing. Harris lost two yards, then lightning struck. Bradshaw dropped deep and hit Swann slanting across from the right to left, just in front of the end line. The six-yard hookup made it 16–10 and Gerela's kick ran it to 17–10 with 11:51 remaining.

Oakland counterpunched from their 15 to the Steeler seven with Stabler's 42-yard pass to Branch the big gainer. Blanda's 24-yard field goal capped the drive with 7:42 to go making it 17–13.

Oakland had a first and ten at its 20 with less than two minutes to play.

Stabler passed for 18 to Branch. Greene sacked Stabler on the next play, but Thomas held downfield. Thomas redeemed himself on the next play, swiping a pass and returning it 37 to the Oakland 24 with one minute left.

Bleier gained three on the first down, then Harris weaved through the middle for 7 and the touchdown that made certain the Steelers would be way down yonder in New Orleans on January 12.

31

First Steelers
Super Bowl Victory

1975

After 42 years, Art Rooney, the beloved owner of the Pittsburgh Steelers, finally had the opportunity to watch his team play for the championship of pro football. After defeating the Oakland Raiders, the Steelers headed to New Orleans to play in Super Bowl IX against the Minnesota Vikings, led by scrambling quarterback Fran Tarkenton. The Steel Curtain defense completely dominated the game and held the Vikings offense to 17 yards rushing and 102 yards passing. They also intercepted three of Tarkenton's passes and tackled him in the end zone for a safety. Leading only 2–0 at halftime, the Steelers, sparked by a record-breaking performance by Franco Harris, named the Super Bowl MVP, and a clutch touchdown pass from Terry Bradshaw, went on to a 16–6 victory. In the Steelers locker room, team captain Andy Russell handed the game ball to a beaming Art Rooney.

SUPER STEELERS WIN, 16–6

Long Wait Ends; Harris is MVP, Sets Rush Mark

January 13, 1975
By David Fink
Pittsburgh Post-Gazette

NEW ORLEANS—The Pittsburgh Steelers chug-a-lugged Minnesota's offense faster than you can say "Pour on the Iron" and whipped the Vikings, 16–6 in Super Bowl IX yesterday.

It was the Steelers' first world championship in 42 years.

Franco Harris, a Sherman tank in a Steeler suit, led the charge with a record 158 yards on 34 rushing attempts.

He was named the game's Most Valuable Player.

Harris scored one touchdown and quarterback Terry Bradshaw passed four yards to tight end Larry Brown for the other. A safety accounted for the Steelers' remaining points.

The Vikings, losing in the Super Bowl for the third time in the last six years, trailed 2–0 at the half and 9–0 at the end of the third quarter. Their lone touchdown came when rookie linebacker Matt Blair blocked a Bobby Walden punt and reserve defensive back Terry Brown covered it in the end zone with 10:33 remaining in the game.

A Key Interception

As was the case in their American Football Conference Championship Game victory over Oakland two weeks ago, the Steelers treated adversity as if it were a gift horse. They drove 66 yards in 11 plays, culminating the retaliatory drive with Bradshaw's short toss to Larry Brown with 3:31 left.

Mike Wagner's interception—the Steelers' third—locked up the win seconds later.

Despite the second-half absence of linebackers Andy Russell and Jack Lambert, Pittsburgh limited the Vikings to only 21 yards rushing on 20 attempts. Meanwhile, the Steelers accumulated 249 yards against Minnesota's willing but weary defense.

Pittsburgh Post-Gazette
Sun-Telegraph
First Newspaper West of the Alleghenies

SUPER STEELERS WIN, 16-6

Long Wait Ends; Harris Is MVP, Sets Rush Mark

Police, Overzealous Fans Clash Downtown

Inside Today's Post-Gazette

Four Years Make a Difference in Harrisburg

The front page of the *Post-Gazette* the day after the Steelers won their first Super Bowl.

Police cars lead the Super Bowl IX champion Steelers through Gateway Center and down Liberty Avenue. (Andy Starnes/*Post-Gazette*)

They did most of their damage to the right as guard Gerry Mullins and tackle Gordon Gravelle caved in the left side of the Vikings once-impenetrable defense.

Quarterback Fran Tarkenton, normally the Vikings' main weapon, passed for only 102 yards. His scrambling was never a factor as Steeler ends L.C. Greenwood and Dwight White repeatedly turned him inside where the traffic was the heaviest.

Steeler Defense Shows

Greenwood also batted down three passes and tackle Ernie Holmes broke up another. Left tackle Joe Greene intercepted a pass as did Wagner and cornerback Mel Blount.

In all, the Vikings turned the ball over five times against the AFC's No. 1 defense.

The win marked the third consecutive time the AFC had triumphed over the NFC champions and it also marked the first time a team playing its first Super Bowl had beaten a team that had played there before.

At first, it was Pittsburgh which seemed doomed to frustration. Twice in the first period, Roy Gerela tried field goals that failed. The first was a 33-yarder that sailed wide. Later, the Steelers tried for a 38-yarder, but a fumbled snap doomed that attempt.

The Vikings, too, tried to get on the scoreboard with a field goal, but Fred Cox's 39-yard attempt also was wide.

The game was developing into a punting duel between Minnesota's Mike Eischeid and Bobby Walden of the Steelers when midway through the second period, the Steeler front four forced a Tarkenton error that led to the 2–0 safety. It was the first safety in Super Bowl history.

With Greene thrusting his arms in the air in celebration, the Pittsburgh fans roared their approval at the front four they call the "Steel Curtain." Tarkenton was to see plenty more of them.

32

Triangles Win
World Team Tennis Title

1975

The original World Team Tennis league lasted only five years, but in its second season, the Pittsburgh Triangles joined the Pirates and the Steelers in giving Pittsburgh a world championship in the 1970s. For the team's first season, the Triangles signed the legendary Ken Rosewall, the brilliant Australian Evonne Goolagong, and the young star, Vitas Gerulaitis. Rosewall left the team after one year, but Googalong and Gerulaitis led the Triangles to the Eastern Division title in its second season with a league's best record of 36–8. After losing the first game of a best-of-three series to the San Francisco Golden Gaters, the Triangles won the next two matches, played at the Civic Arena, and clamed the Bancroft Cup. The 21-year-old, Gerulaitis was named the Most Valuable Player in the play-offs. The Triangles success on the tennis court didn't lead to success at the box office, and the team folded after its third season.

MIGHTY TRI'S CAPTURE WTT TITLE

Close Door on Golden Gaters, 21–14

August 26, 1975
By Vince Leonard
Pittsburgh Post-Gazette

They're hardly as ferocious but add the Triangles to the Steelers in Pittsburgh world champions in 1975.

Ferocious no, gutty yes.

And exemplified by the slightest member, Vitas Gerulaitis at 6–1 and 155, who demolished Tom Okker 6–1 in the fourth event on a night scheduled for five.

The Triangles beat the Golden Gaters of San Francisco 21–14 in a terminated match halted when the Gaters were mathematically overwhelmed.

Even the final was a football score, but the overall effort was achieved by finesse. And 6,882 fans gave the Pittsburghers a standing ovation when it was over.

Also, when it was over Gerulaitis earned Most Valuable Player honors from the league and the Triangles the Bancroft Cup, symbolic of World Team Tennis supremacy.

"It's great," said Gerulaitis of the MVP award. "What can I say: I wanted to win it."

Gerulaitis had heaps of assistance.

Evonne Goolagong, the princess-like performer for the Triangles, turned a 2–6 deficit into an 8–8 tie after beating Betty Stove in singles.

"I felt I had to win as many games as possible," Goolagong said of her must-win singles set. "I was pretty determined not to lose after the doubles."

Goolagong ranked the WTT championship as just below the Federation Cup in team achievement. "This would be close to it," Goolagong said.

Gerulaitis swiped a page from Goolagong's ledger by turning in twin wins, teaming with Mark Cox to handle Frew McMillan and Tom Okker in doubles.

"This is a great team. Whoever says tennis is not a team sport is ridiculous. Team morale won the competition tonight in particular and the playoffs in general."

The Triangles, who also posted the Eastern Division championship along the way with a 32–8 record, notched a 4–1 effort in playoffs.

"It's simply great," said Coach Vic Edwards. "It had been the only championship my pupils hadn't won up until now in tennis."

Gerulaitis, who disposed of Okker on points 21–14 as well as the whopping five-game margin, was asked if he ever had an easier time of it.

"Hey are you kidding?" the ebullient Lithuanian shot back. "Every point was like pulling teeth. I went for the second service rather than pussy-footing around with it."

The four points that beat Okker and won the championship went like this: 0–1 as Vitas hit into the net: 1–1 on Vitas' passing shot: 2–1 on another passing shot: 3–1 as Okker hit into the net: and 4–1 as Okker returned beyond the baseline.

Asked how it ranked with his other tennis achievements, Gerulaitis said, "It's up there because I'm sharing it with six people.

"It was a nice finish. A lot of people said bad things about our men players, but the men won the championship.

"We won all the doubles and one of two in singles."

And owner Frank Fuhrer, in a piece de resistance, donned the sweatshirt of the Gerulaitis fan club, The G-Men, changed into a suit at mid-match, then back into the sweatshirt so he might willingly be tossed into the shower.

The Triangles went on intermission with a hard-earned 15–13 lead, highlighted by a half dozen ties and Goolagong's startling turnabout work.

Stove and Kloss bettered the Triangles distaff stars, 6–2, in a set that featured five sudden deaths in eight games. The Gaters grabbed a 1–0 lead, breaking Michel's service, and increased the margin inexorably.

Goolagong and Stove stayed up front to battle each other and it was Evonne despite great play by the tall Hollander. First service difficulties by Goolagong notwithstanding, the Aussie superstar kept things under control and notched six of the eight games to pull the Triangles from four games down into an 8–8 tie.

At that point, Cox and Gerulaitis met Okker and McMillan head-on and the virile quartet gave the fans something to cheer about.

Employing a two-handed backhand and sharp side shots, the white-capped McMillan played absolutely brilliant tennis but got little help from Okker. Gerulaitis led the way and was ably backed by Cox, as both turned in some beautiful shooting.

Pittsburgh won the men's doubles, 7–5 grabbing the leads, 1–0, then tied with the Golden Gaters in games 1–1, 2–2, 3–3, 4–4, and 5–5.

Tremendous individual shots titillated the crowd, but in the end, it was the teamwork of Mark and Vitas that accounted for the last two games and their sixth straight doubles win over Okker and McMillan.

33

Steelers Super Bowl Victory over the Dallas Cowboys

1976

After breezing through the 1975 regular schedule and defeating the Baltimore Colts in the first round of the playoffs, the Steelers faced their nemeses again for the AFC championship. In a freezing rain that turned Three Rivers Stadium into an ice bowl, the Steelers edged the Raiders 17–10 and headed to Miami for Super Bowl X. With the chance to become only the third team to win back-to-back Super Bowls, the Steelers faced the Dallas Cowboys and quarterback Roger Staubach.

Trailing 10–7 going into the fourth quarter, the Steelers surged ahead 15–10 on a safety and two field goals, but the game-winning play was yet to come. With barely three minutes left in the game, Terry Bradshaw threw a 62-yard touchdown pass to Lynn Swann, and the Steelers, after a desperate Cowboys rally, were able to hang on for a 21–17 victory. Lynn Swann caught four passes for 161 yards in the game and was named the Super Bowl MVP.

SUPER STEELERS SHATTER COWBOYS

January 19, 1976
By Vito Stellino
Pittsburgh Post-Gazette

MIAMI—Forget the Monsters of the Midway. Forget Run to Daylight. Forget the No-Name Defense.

Forget the 1958 Baltimore–New York overtime game. Forget the 1967 Dallas–Green Bay Ice Bowl. Forget last year's Oakland-Miami playoff game.

Remember instead, the Pittsburgh Steelers. And remember their 21–17 victory over the Dallas Cowboys in Super Bowl X.

It was a game to remember. And the Steelers are a team to remember.

They've now won two straight Super Bowls. Only Green Bay and Miami have matched that. Now they're going for three straight.

The Steelers showed they're champions yesterday. They showed they can win any way they have to. They showed a sellout crowd of 80,187 at the Orange Bowl and millions more on television that they're a team for the ages.

They showed the Super Bowl doesn't have to be a conservative, defense-oriented game. The Steelers and the Cowboys both came to stage a shootout. The loser was going to go down with guns blazing.

The Steelers passed for a touchdown on third-and-1. They tried another pass and failed on fourth-and-2.

It wound up with Roger Staubach firing into the end zone on the final play of the game with everything up for grabs. But Glen Edwards intercepted it to end the most exciting Super Bowl ever and one of the most dramatic championship games of all time.

In the end, the Steelers proved they deserve to be champions. They're champions because Lynn Swann came back from a concussion to show he still has those hands that would make a pickpocket seem clumsy.

They're the champions because Roy Gerela, whose ribs hurt so badly that he sighed as he drew each breath after the game, came back from missing two earlier field goals to kick a pair of pressure-packed ones in the final period.

Front page of the January 19, 1976, *Post-Gazette* after the Steelers whip Dallas in Super Bowl X.

They're the champions because Terry Bradshaw proved he's a winning quarterback who was able to throw the winning touchdown pass even though he was clobbered as he released the ball and didn't even know if went for a score.

They're the champions because all 43 guys play an important role, even the unsung special team guys like Reggie Harrison, who blocked a punt that turned the game around in the fourth period.

They're the champions because Chuck Noll, a guy who usually plays it tight-to-the-vest, seemed like a swashbuckling riverboat gambler as he took several big chances and came out on top.

They're the champions because Randy Grossman caught a touchdown pass on a play the club hadn't used since the College All-Star game.

Yes, the Steelers are the champions.

How good are they now? Do they rank with the great teams?

"Those other great teams are gone and we're still trying to reach our peak," grinned Mel Blount.

"I don't like the word 'dynasty,'" said Andy Russell. "We don't win things for that. We win for today. But I'll say one thing. The pro football being played today is the best that's ever been played. It's a lot better than when I came into the league 13 years ago. And we're the champions. So draw your own conclusions."

The Steelers played their usual tough physical game and Jack Lambert became quite upset when Cliff Harris taunted Gerela after a missed field goal. Lambert stepped in to jaw with Harris and tempers flared. The Steelers, who sacked Roger Staubach seven times for a Super Bowl record, didn't have a single penalty called on them.

But they weren't exactly super at the start. They got fooled on a reverse on the opening kickoff and Gerela bruised his ribs making the tackle that probably was responsible for his missed field goals.

Then Bobby Walden fumbled the snap on a punt and the Steelers' defense then got caught by a Dallas shift. Half the defense was playing one defense, the other half was playing another and the result was a 29-yard touchdown pass by Staubach to Drew Pearson for the 7–0 lead in the first period. It was the first time all year the Steelers have given up a touchdown in the first period.

The Steelers came right back to tie it up, thanks largely to the first circus catch by Swann and a surprise play when Bradshaw flipped the seven-yard touchdown pass to Grossman on a third-and-1 call when the Steelers were in their tight-end, short-yard running offense.

Toni Fritsch's 36-yard field goal with 36 seconds elapsed in the second period was the next score and it stayed that way until the final period. By this time, there were a lot of nervous Steeler fans in the stands and back in the front of their TV sets in Pittsburgh.

The Steelers seemed to be dominating the game, but Gerela had missed two field goals and the Steelers couldn't crack the goal line.

Then came the big play. The Steelers had Dallas in a fourth-and-13 situation on the Cowboy 16 and they decided to try and block the punt. Dave Brown played up close to create a 10-men rush instead of dropping back and Dallas didn't adjust its blocking.

The path opened for Harrison to crash though and he blocked Mitch Hoopes' punt out of the end zone for the safety that made it 10–9. "I just wish that ball hadn't bounced out of the end zone and I could have fallen on it for six," Brown said.

The game seemed to turn around.

After Dallas kicked off, the Steelers marched back to the Dallas 20. Gerela came in to try a 36-yarder with 8:41 left in the game.

A lot of Pittsburgh people were thinking about Carson Long as Gerela went to try the third one after missing two. The fact that his ribs were aching didn't help, either.

"I wasn't worried," Gerela said in the locker room with the pain openly showing in his face. "I hadn't missed the other two by much. It wasn't like I was way off."

Gerela got it through and the Steelers were ahead, 12–10, for the first time in the game. He added an 18-yarder and Bradshaw hit Swann on the 64-yard touchdown strike as Dallas gambled on a safety blitz that failed.

Bradshaw went down on the play and was still dazed after the game, but the score was 21–10 as Gerela's extra point attempt hit the crossbar.

Then came the Dallas charge. Staubach's touchdown pass to Percy Howard cut the deficit to 21–17, and their last attempt came after they took over on their own 39 with 1:22 left.

Noll's decision to run the ball on the fourth down instead of trying to punt drew a lot of questions after the game.

"We already had botched one punt and they can score a touchdown on a blocked punt," Noll said. "I had confidence in our defense. We were giving them the ball with no timeouts and I figured our defense could do it."

It did.

Mike Wagner had already intercepted a pass that set up Gerela's second field goal when he recognized a Dallas formation out of the shotgun and stepped in front of Drew Pearson.

Staubach scrambled once and tossed a few passes but the best he could do was to get to the Steelers' 38.

Those 38 yards looked like a short distance to the writers who were standing in the end zone on the way to the dressing room for interview with the Steelers ahead by 11.

But Glen Edwards intercepted a pass to end the game. On the play before that, Howard was hit at about the 5, and as the ball went over his head he protested to no avail that interference should have been called.

"It was tough at the end with no timeouts left," Staubach said.

But as Lee Roy Jordan said, "I'm proud of the way this team played."

The Steelers could be proud, too.

Franco Harris said, "I'm very happy, more excited than last year. We're No. 1 two times…we have championship blood in us."

The Steelers certainly do.

34

Tony Dorsett Breaks NCAA Rushing Record against Navy

1976

The first thing Johnny Majors did when he arrived in Pittsburgh after accepting the head football coaching job at Pitt was to visit Hopewell High School in Aliquippa. He knew that his first step in bringing Pitt back to national prominence, after a dismal 1–10 finish in 1972, was to recruit Tony Dorsett. After being courted by the likes of Ohio State's Woody Hayes and Penn State's Joe Paterno, Dorsett decided to enroll at Pitt and, in his freshman year, ran for 1,586 yards. He became the first player to run for more than a thousand yards in all four of his varsity seasons, and, by the seventh game of his senior year, was poised to become college football's all-time leading rusher by eclipsing Archie Griffin's record of 5,177 yards in four years at Ohio State. Carrying the ball for 180 yards in a 42–0 victory over Navy, Dorsett broke Griffin's record on his last carry of the game, a 32-yard touchdown run.

DORSETT GRABS A CHUNK OF HISTORY

October 25, 1976
By Phil Axelrod
Pittsburgh Post-Gazette

ANNAPOLIS, MARYLAND—Standing in the cement runway and pressed against the wall by a horde of newsmen shoving microphones in his face, Tony Dorsett lifted his eyes and looked at the metallic plaques hanging overhead that honored Navy's war heroes.

He immediately caught the quintessence of the historic moment shortly after Pitt thrashed Navy, 45–0.

"Those were great men who made history," said Dorsett. "Today, I made history, but I don't consider myself to be a great man."

On this cool, brisk Saturday afternoon with the sun sinking slowly, Dorsett was basking in the glory of breaking Archie Griffin's NCAA major college career rushing record of 5,177 yards.

Historians and trivia buffs will make note that at 4:05 PM with 13:22 showing on the fourth quarter scoreboard clock, Dorsett took the pitch from quarterback Tom Yewcic, circled left end to avoid a couple of would-be tacklers, and sped into the end zone for a spectacular 32-yard touchdown.

The run set off an explosion of human emotion as Pitt's entire bench cleared in a spontaneous display of affection and mobbed Dorsett. He made it off the field, where he was met by his mother, Myrtle, and father, Wes, who embraced in a tearful scene.

"I was so emotionally high it was unbelievable," said Dorsett, admitting his eyes moistened at the time. "We all cried and loved it to death. She was so happy, tears just had to drop out of my eyes."

The crowd of 26,346 rose in unison for a standing ovation while the Navy band hailed Dorsett with a one-gun salute.

On a day waxed with feelings, statistics seemed a rather mundane exercise, but, nevertheless, it is relevant to note Dorsett's record-breaking accomplishments.

His 180 yards rushing gave him 5,206 career yards, shattering Griffin's mark; his 1,072 yards so far this season make him the first runner in the history of college football to rush for 1,000 or more yards in four season; and his 27 carries gave him 930 for his career, pushing him past Ed Marinaro's NCAA record number 918.

Dorsett is still 91 yards shy of 5,297 yards gained by Howard Stevens, who played two years at Randolph-Macon, a small college in Virginia, and two years at Louisville. Steven's total is not recognized officially, however, as either a major or small-college record.

"I'm hoping I can push that record up so far no one can ever dream of beating it," said Dorsett, cocking his head back and grinning. "Maybe they can hope for No. 2, but I want that record to be mine as long as I'm on this earth."

President Gerald Ford meets Pitt Panthers football star Tony Dorsett at Greater Pittsburgh International Airport. (Albert Hermann Jr./*Post-Gazette*)

With four regular-season games to go, Dorsett would like to reach the 6,000-yard plateau, a goal well within his reach. Against Navy, he upped his 100-yard string to 14 in a row and 29 for his career, four short of Griffin's record of 33.

"This record was so exciting for me because my teammates wanted it so badly for me," said Dorsett, who thanked them all in a closed locker room session.

However, Pitt's exuberance cost the Panthers a 15-yard penalty as they poured onto the field. "That's the happiest penalty I've ever had a team get in my life," said Johnny Majors. "This couldn't happen to a better young man and a great football player."

Majors turned to Dorsett and said, "Tony Dorsett, you're the greatest football player in America and the greatest football player I've ever seen."

Losing coach George Welsh added, "I've said before he's in a class by himself. O.J. Simpson is the only one I've seen who comes close."

Dorsett broke the record with flair, just the way he said he was going to do it.

"I planned it that way and I'm fortunate it happened that way," he said, grinning. "I told Mom this is the happiest day of my life."

Dorsett smiled. "I wanted to do a little dance in the end zone," he said, adding he practiced a routine all week, "but I didn't get the chance. I wanted to do some showboating."

Dorsett's teammates, to a man, said they shared in the record, particularly the offensive linemen.

"I'm just proud to be able to say that I blocked for the greatest runner in the history of football," said center John Pelusi. "It's always been easy to block for Tony. With Tony on your side, it's like playing 13 against 11."

Added John Hanhauser, "He's like a racehorse out there. I've never seen him tired this year." On a serious note, he continued, "I feel that I'm part of every one of those yards. I think Tony's the first to admit he needs our help."

Another guy giving Dorsett help has been Elliott Walker. "I help by blocking and by running. I take off some of the pressure," he said. "I'm just real happy to be playing next to the guy who's going to win the Heisman Trophy."

When Dorsett finally finished, signing autographs and answering questions, he slowly left the locker room where he was greeted by a lilting, melodious chorus set to "Jesus Christ, Superstar."

As sung by joyous Pitt students, it went, "Tony Dorsett, Superstar, who the Hell do you think you are?"

The greatest running back in the history of college football, that's who Tony Dorsett is.

35

Pitt Defeats Georgia in Sugar Bowl and Captures National Championship

1977

In 1976 Pitt completed its first unde-feated regular season since 1937 with a convincing 27–3 win over Penn State in a nationally televised game played at Three Rivers Stadium. Tony Dorsett ran for 224 yards and two touchdowns and broke Ed Marinaro's single-season rush-ing record and Glenn Davis' record for most points in a career. Ranked No. 1 in the country, Pitt played in the Sugar Bowl against the Georgia Bulldogs on New Year's Day for the national title. Georgia's "junkyard dogs' were no match for Pitt's of-fense, and the Panthers breezed to a 27–3 victory and its first national championship since 1937. Dorsett rushed for 202 yards and a touch-down, but Matt Cavanaugh with 192 yards passing and a touchdown run-ning and passing was named the Sugar Bowl MVP. It was the last game for Johnny Majors who had accepted an offer to coach at his alma mater, the University of Tennessee.

THE PARTY LINE: ONE CHAMP, IT'S PITT

January 3, 1977
By Marino Parascenzo
Pittsburgh Post-Gazette

NEW ORLEANS—They gave a No. 1 party, and no one came. Not Woody, not Bo, and not John. Some said not Georgia and its Junkyard Dogs, either.

And wouldn't you know it?—no champagne, either.

Not much of a party spirit, for that matter. The Pitt Panthers trotted back to their dressing room to nothing wetter than a hot shower, wearing so-whats on their faces. Could this be the football team that had just won the national championship?

Well, it truly was all over but the election. The landslide had already taken place. Georgia's Bulldogs had just been buried on the Superdome turf, 27–3, in the 1977 Sugar Bowl. It hardly mattered that on a crisp Saturday New Year's afternoon, the Orange and Rose Bowls still had to be played.

Woody Hayes of Ohio State, angry at something, deduced that Pitt chose the Sugar in order to avoid playing the Colorado team he would meet. And in Pasadena, Bo Schembechler of Michigan and John Robinson of Southern Cal proclaimed that their Rose Bowl game would decide the national title, no matter what the rest of the country said.

Al Romano, Pitt middle guard, had his solution. "Did the Rose Bowl start yet?" he said, bending to cut the tape from his ankles. "No? Well, go tell them to call it off. Tell them not to bother."

Pitt entered the Sugar Bowl No. 1 in both wire service polls. And when you've stepped out of the Sugar like a puppy coming from a card house, and you've left No. 5 Georgia 10–2 and gasping in their own wreckage, why, all you need is the National Broadcasting Company to anoint you.

The official word on the unofficial national championship should be forthcoming shortly from the wire services. Meanwhile the question remains, which play worked best—Dorsett off tackle, Cavanaugh-to-whoever, or a sweep through the French Quarter?

University of Pittsburgh QB Matt Cavanaugh carries the Sugar Bowl MVP trophy as the Panthers arrive at the airport fresh from their trouncing of Georgia. From left: Mayor Pete Flaherty, Cavanaugh, Jim Flaherty, Jackie Sherrill, and Laverga Walker. (Morris Berman/ *Post-Gazette*)

They've quit telling ethnic jokes in New Orleans. Now it's Pitt jokes. "The Georgia players are now in bed," said one television guy on the 11 PM news, "and Pitt is just getting dressed up to go out." "Majors posted a curfew," another gag went. "He told them to be in by February."

It all began when Southern media people went pale when they learned that Johnny Majors, author of Pitt's success and now officially the Tennessee coach, let his players maintain their on-campus lifestyle. Which meant no curfews until a couple of days before the game, and freedom to roam. At the same time, Georgia's players were being bed-checked at something like 10:30 or 11.

Contrary to popular belief, both Biloxi, Mississippi, site of the first week's drills, and the French Quarter were still there at last look.

The Panthers, at first surprised by the reaction, missed few chances to embellish the notion they were the big partying team out of the effete East.

Defensive tackle Don Parrish, for example, was limping toward the locker room on his sprained ankle. Someone wanted to know whether it was serious. "Oh, it will be all right," Parrish said, "soon as I have a couple drinks."

After the game, a Georgia fan at the Pitt hotel headquarters, noting the Georgia curfew, lifted his hands and sighed. "So much for clean living."

The game was over quickly. Pitt struck for a 21–3 lead in the first half—quarterback Matt Cavanaugh trotting six yards for the first touchdown, hitting receiver Gordon Jones on a 59-yard pass play for the second score, and Tony Dorsett swishing 11 yards for the third. Then, aside from two field goals by Carson Long, Pitt sat in the second half. "We wanted to eat up the clock," Majors said. Get it over with, he meant.

The Panthers had to survive not only the nightlife, but also a bout of virus that put down about eight players and four children accompanying the team as well as the boisterous nagging of Georgia fans.

A large contingent lodged at the Marriott where the Pitt team stayed. What started as good fun degenerated into harassment Pitt players found barely bearable. One night, a lobby mob refused to part and let Dorsett and tight end Jim Corbett reach the elevators.

At the Superdome, it was Pitt's turn. While Dorsett was rushing to a Sugar Bowl record of 202 yards and Cavanaugh was picking up the Most Valuable Player Award, the Pitt people joked.

The jokes were perfectly awful. "It's a dog's life." "Their bark is more worse than their bite." "They're more bull than dog." Like that. But they had a kind of healing effect on the sores of that pre-game abuse.

What was happening was that Georgia's 1,000-yard rusher, Kevin McLee of Uniontown, Pennsylvania, was kept busy getting 48 yards in his 14 carries. And quarterback Ray Goff, the Southeastern Conference's player of the year, who had 724 for the year, got 76. Goff and three other Bulldogs quarterbacks got off a total of 22 passes. Three were completed to Georgia guys and four to Pitt guys. Pitt also took in two fumbles, improving on its average of four turnovers per game.

The tale is complete in Sugar's profit-and-loss statement. The Georgia offense had averaged 335 yards and 29 points per game. It got 181 and 3. The Junkyard dog defense had allowed averages of 271 yards and 10 points. It gave up 480 and 27.

One of the Georgia quarterbacks was Tony Flanagan, 6–3 sophomore who is also a standout on the Georgia basketball team. Dooley called on Flanagan midway through the fourth quarter to get something started. Anything. Flanagan dropped back to pass on his first play, and was crushed for an eight-yard loss by Pitt defensive tackle Randy Holloway.

It was a clumsy social moment for Holloway. He and Flanagan had become friends playing together in an all-star basketball tournament in Sharon, Pennsylvania, some years earlier. What do you say to an old friend you just planted?

"Well, uh..." Holloway paused, embarrassed. "I said, well, uh, 'Hello Tony.'"

Flanagan wasn't invited to the postgame party. It wasn't a farewell party thrown by Majors, who left early yesterday for Hawaii and the Hula Bowl with Dorsett, Romano, and Corbett. It was a welcome party thrown by Jackie Sherrill, the new Pitt coach. Well, at least he was off to the right start.

36

Steelers Super Bowl Victory over the Dallas Cowboys

1979

After winning two straight Super Bowls, the Steelers struggled with injuries and were eliminated in the playoffs for the next two years. They bounced back in 1978 and ended with a 14–2 regular season record, the best in team history. They dominated the Denver Broncos and the Houston Oilers in the playoffs and headed back to Miami for a rematch with the Dallas Cowboys. In their first two Super Bowl seasons, the Steel Curtain defense and the running of Franco Harris led the Steelers, but 1978 was the year of Terry Bradshaw. He passed for 28 touchdowns, ten more than his previous high, and was named the Steelers MVP and the NFL Player of the Year. Despite the pregame taunting of Cowboys linebacker Thomas "Hollywood" Henderson, Bradshaw dominated Super Bowl XIII. He threw for 318 yards and four touchdowns in a 35–31 Steelers victory and was the unanimous choice for Super Bowl MVP. A late Dallas rally made the score close, but the Steelers, not the Cowboys, became the first NFL team to win three Super Bowls.

SUPER, SUPER, SUPER

Bradshaw's 4 TD Passes Set Record

January 22, 1979
By Vito Stellino
Pittsburgh Post-Gazette

MIAMI—Light up the skies. Beat the drums. Let the words ring out.

The Pittsburgh Steelers are a team for the ages and Terry Bradshaw is a quarterback for any era.

The Steelers carved their niche in the pro football history books yesterday by becoming the first team to win three Super Bowls.

Before 78,656 fans in the Orange Bowl—many of them Steeler partisans waving their "Terrible Towels"—the Steelers whipped the Dallas Cowboys 35–31 in Super Bowl XIII in a game that wasn't as close as the score sounded.

Putting a football in Terry Bradshaw's hands is like handing Picasso a brush or Hemingway a pen. He riddled the Cowboys for 318 yards and four touchdowns in the best day of his pro career.

That enabled the Steelers to become the "team of the 70s" by winning their third championship in five years. Only the Green Bay Packers, who won five titles in seven years in the 1960s (three of them before the Super Bowl was founded), have surpassed the Steelers.

But that was a different era and the Steelers feel they have established themselves as the best football team ever to play the game.

"We'd have Ray Nitschke (the celebrated Green Bay middle linebacker) and those guys for lunch," boasted Dwight White.

Jack Ham, a man not give to extravagant claims, said simply, "This is the best football team I've ever seen."

The way the Steelers rolled through the playoffs was awe-inspiring. They got one point better with each game.

They beat Denver 33–10, Houston 34–5, and had a 35–17 lead on Dallas in the fourth period before the Cowboys scored two late touchdowns to make it close.

The Steelers finished pro football's longest season with a 17–2 record for a

**Phil Musick:
Bradshaw's
Finest Hour
Page 21**

**Bradshaw
Voted Most
Valuable
Player**

**Joe Greene:
Third Title
Not the Last
Page 21**

Pittsburgh Post-Gazette

FINAL
EDITION

VOL. 52—NO. 150   In Three Sections   MONDAY, JANUARY 22, 1979   15 CENTS

Super Super Super

Iran Council May Lose 2 To Pressure

By ERIC PACE

Bradshaw's 4 TD Passes Set Record

By VITO STELLINO

Steelers' Coach Chuck Noll is carried off the field in triumph after the win. Steelers showing elation are Rick Moore, L., and Joe Greene, r.

Jubilant Steeler Fans Fail to Conquer City

(Continued on Page 4, Column 1)
(Continued on Page 6, Column 1)
(Continued on Page 11, Column 3)

Today

The Pothole Plague

Too Many Rules

Today's Quote

Budget Day

Pluto's Progress

Back to Work

Rabies Shots

A New Life

By DAVID WAGNER

percentage topped in modern times only by Miami's 17–0 mark in 1972 and Green Bay's 14–1 mark in 1962.

Dallas, becoming the second team to lose three Super Bowls (Minnesota has lost four), finished at 14–5.

Although Bradshaw overcame an interception and two fumbles to win the MVP award, it wasn't a one-man show.

The Steelers, who have 22 veterans from their first Super Bowl team, showed they're champions for a lot of reasons.

They're champions because they have an offensive line that neutralized the vaunted Dallas defensive line.

They're the champions because they have a pair of receivers named Lynn Swann and John Stallworth, who burned the Dallas cornerbacks time and time again.

They're champions because they have a defense that can still make the big play and dominate a game.

They're the champions because they have a blocking back named Rocky Bleier, who plays in the shadow but can come up with a crucial touchdown catch.

They're champions because Franco Harris can be bottled up for much of the game and then break a critical play.

But it all comes back to Bradshaw. It is not enough to say he's the best quarterback playing the game. You have to look back at people like Unitas and Starr and Layne and Graham when you talk about him.

"I told Bradshaw he had a hell of a game," Dallas' Cliff Harris said. "You don't psyche him."

There was a lot of talking during the week and Bradshaw did none of it. He just did the playing. He fell behind 14–7 in the second period after Mike Hegman pulled a ball from his arms and ran 37 yards for a Dallas touchdown.

A lesser quarterback might have been rattled. Not Terry Bradshaw. "It's the mark of the maturity of the man," Joe Greene marveled.

Bradshaw put two more touchdowns on the board in the first half for a 21–14 lead. When Dallas cut the lead to 21–17 and Pittsburgh was held to one first down in the third quarter, a lesser quarterback might have been rattled again. But not Bradshaw. He drove the team 85 yards in the fourth quarter for the touchdown that broke the Cowboys' back.

When the Steeler offense took the field with 12:08 left in the game, the situation looked critical. The Steelers were ahead, 21–17, but they had the lead only because Jackie Smith had dropped a sure touchdown pass in the end zone. The Cowboys settled for a field goal.

The Steelers had not moved the ball in the second half. "In the huddle, guys were saying, 'We've got to go 85 (yards)...we've got to go 85,'" John Kolb noted.

They went 85.

"Chuck (Noll) wasn't conservative," Bradshaw said, explaining the third quarter lag. "We knew they'd change their coverages. I wanted to take my time."

Time was running out, Kolb said. "We knew we couldn't tread water with Dallas. We were conscious of the fact that if we didn't make something happen, Dallas would. If we had one fault all year, it was that when we got ahead, we didn't knock out teams."

The Steelers went ahead for the knockout. Bradshaw hit Randy Grossman for nine yards. He hit Lynn Swann for 13. Franco Harris went for five yards. Then Benny Barnes was called for tripping Swann, producing a 33-yard penalty. Barnes protested the most controversial call of the game.

Four plays later, Bradshaw faced a third-and-nine on the Dallas 22. The Cowboys were looking for the pass. Bradshaw called a tackle trap play.

"We caught 'em blitzing, and there was a really nice hole," Franco said.

The run was poetic justice. On the previous play, Harris jawed with Thomas Henderson. Henderson tackled Bradshaw after the whistle had blown when the Steelers were called for too much time.

"I wish we could say we planned it that way," Greene said.

With a 28–17 lead, the Steelers had a seemingly comfortable margin. Dirt Winston recovered a fumble on the ensuing kickoff and Bradshaw fired an 18-yard strike to Swann to wrap it up.

Dallas scored two touchdowns to make it closer and make the bettors sweat, but the game was decided.

It was close and exciting enough to leave Dallas with a lot of "what ifs?" What if Tom Landry had run Dorsett more? He got 38 yards on his first three carries and carried only 12 times the rest of the game. Landry's call for a reverse that turned into a fumble killing the first drive also was puzzling. The tripping penalty on Barnes also caused much consternation in Dallas.

The Steelers were simply the better team. Three years ago, the same teams did the same thing and the Steelers won by four points, 21–17.

They were better then and they're better now. After two frustrating years, the Steelers are back on top.

"It's taken all year to prove we're the best team," Loren Toews said.

They have proved it. Without a doubt.

They're the Super Steelers. Super Steelers III.

37

Pirates World Series Victory over the Baltimore Orioles

1979

After winning the 1971 World Series, the Pirates returned to the National League playoffs in 1972, 1974, and 1975, but lost each time. In 1979 they were back in the playoffs and played the Cincinnati Reds. The Reds had defeated the Pirates in the 1972 and 1975 playoffs, but this time the Pirates, led by Willie Stargell, swept the Reds in three games and went on to the World Series. As in the 1971 World Series, the Pirates' opponent was a heavily favored Baltimore Orioles team, and, though the plot was different and most of the cast of characters had changed, the ending was the same. The Pirates, trailing the Orioles three games to one, fought back to tie the World Series. They won the seventh and deciding game in Baltimore, just as they had in 1971, on a home run by a future Hall of Fame Pirate who had turned the series into his personal showcase. It was the year of "Pops" Stargell and the Pirates "fam-i-lee."

BATTLIN' BUCS BEAT 'EM

4–1 Victory Caps Series Comeback

October 18, 1979
By Charley Feeney
Pittsburgh Post-Gazette

BALTIMORE—One time it was Bill Mazeroski. Another time it was Roberto Clemente and Steve Blass. This time it was Willie Stargell.

Wonderful Willie, 38 years young, carried the Pirates with his bat last night and led the bounce-back Buccos to baseball's world championship with a dramatic 4–1 win over the Baltimore Orioles.

Stargell, named the Most Valuable Player of the Series, was the only Pirate in the seven games to produce a home run. He hit his third last night against Scott McGregor. It was a two-run blast over the right-field wall, wiping out a 1–0 Baltimore lead.

Rich Dauer's third-inning homer off Pirate starter Jimmy Bibby accounted for the Baltimore run.

A crowd of 53,733, including President Carter, saw Stargell collect four hits, a single and two doubles to go with his homer. Later, President Carter went to the Pirates' clubhouse to congratulate the Pirates.

Four clubs have come back in the Series after being down, three games to one. The Pirates are the only team to do it twice.

The 1925 Pirates rallied to beat the Washington Senators. The 1958 New York Yankees won the last three games over the Milwaukee Braves and the 1968 Detroit Tigers did it against the St. Louis Cardinals.

Through the tense, dramatic comeback that started with a 7–1 win in Pittsburgh Sunday, Chuck Tanner managed with the knowledge that his mother had died.

The Pirates stayed alive with a 4–0 victory Tuesday night here. Each time, the Pirate starter appeared overmatched. Jim Rooker went against 23-game winner Mike Flanagan Sunday. John Candelaria went against veteran Jim Palmer Tuesday night and Bibby last night faced McGregor, the Baltimore left-hander, who was an 8–4 winner in the third game.

Stargell said that President Carter congratulated him, and Willie, smiling, later said: "I was going to ask him for some peanuts, but there were a lot of security guards around."

Stargell said he spoke with batting coach Bob Skinner in the fifth inning. "The one thing I didn't want was to stay too close if he (McGregor) threw me a fastball."

Bill Robinson punched a single past shortstop Kiko Garcia with one out in the sixth before Stargell drove his homer over the wall near the Pirates' bullpen.

Chuck Tanner said when Stargell went to the plate in the sixth, some players on the bench shouted: "Come on Pops, get it going,"

"I didn't hear anything," Stargell said. "I was concentrating on McGregor. I didn't hit the ball good the first two times up."

Pirates' manager Chuck Tanner savors the World Series championship trophy on his ride home. (Edwin Morgan/ *Post-Gazette*)

Stargell got a bloop single to left in the second inning and a pop fly double to left in the fourth.

Stargell said signing his first pro contract for $1,500 was one of the greatest thrills.

"And tonight...this one belongs, too," he said.

Later Stargell left his emotions out in the open. He hugged his sister and he was crying.

Stargell played in the 1971 World Series and batted under .220. He scored the winning run in Blass' seventh-game victory.

In this Series, he was 12-for-30 and set a Series record with seven extra-base hits.

The Orioles almost pulled the game out in the eighth, and when they failed, the Pirates scored two runs in the ninth to sew up this 76th World Series.

Bibby, who left for a pinch hitter in the fifth, was replaced by Don Robinson, who has some soreness in the right shoulder after working three games in relief. But he told Tanner he could pitch.

Baltimore's Doug DeCinces is out at second in front of the Pirates Phil Garner after a 5th-inning double play. (Darrell Sapp/*Post-Gazette*)

Robinson gave up a leadoff single to Doug DeCinces, and with two out, he walked McGregor. Grant Jackson relieved and got Al Bumbry on a pop to Bill Madlock.

Jackson breezed until he walked pinch-hitter Lee May with one out in the eighth. When Jackson, who was the winning pitcher, walked Bumbry, Kent Tekulve relieved.

The Baltimore fans were shouting.

They remembered that the Birds rallied to beat Tekulve in a six-run eighth inning in the fourth game. They tried to forget that Tekulve had been effective in his other three relief jobs in the Series.

Tekulve retired Terry Crowley, a pinch-hitter, on a hopper to Phil Garner as the runners advanced.

Ken Singleton was walked intentionally, filling the bases for Eddie Murray, who was 0-for-20. Murray hit a Tekulve pitch hard, but it was a liner to right. Dave Parker stumbled while backtracking, but made the catch.

Baltimore manager Earl Weaver, who said he thought the Orioles had the Series won after they went ahead three to one last Saturday, used five pitchers, a Series record, in the ninth when the Pirates scored their cushion runs.

Omar Moreno, who had a great bat ending after a poor start, singled across Garner, who opened with a double off Tim Stoddard. Moreno's hit came off Flanagan, the Birds' 23-game winner who won the first game and lost the fifth game.

Later in the inning, Dennis Martinez hit Bill Robinson with a pitch with the bases loaded to produce the fourth run.

Garner's bat sizzled through the 10 postseason games, including the playoffs. He ended the season with a 14-game hitting streak and stretched it to a 24-game streak in October.

Garner would have been the Series MVP, winning the car awarded by a magazine, but old Pops Stargell took it away from him with his seventh-game dramatics.

Tekulve didn't give the Pirate fans any anxious moments in the ninth. He struck out Gary Roenicke and DeCinces and got pinch-hitter Pat Kelly on a fly ball to Moreno in center.

"I didn't see Moreno make the catch," Tekulve said. "I knew he had it."

As Moreno clutched the last out, the Pirates started celebrating. Tanner walked to a box seat next to the Pirate dugout and shook hands with National League President Chub Feeney, who had watched the American League Yankees win the last two World Series from the Los Angeles Dodgers.

Tanner will bury his mother today in New Castle. The personal heartache was beginning to show on the 50-year-old manager.

"The team won it," Tanner said. "Willie Stargell played like a 25-year-old."

Now Stargell joins Mazeroski, whose ninth-inning homer in 1960 beat the Yankees, and Clemente and Blass, whose bat and right arm won the 1971 Series against the Orioles.

Willie was magnificent. The Pirates were great in their comeback.

38

Steelers Super Bowl Victory over the Los Angeles Rams

1980

In December 1979, the Steelers ended any doubt that they were the NFL team of the decade when they crushed the Miami Dolphins, the dominant team of the early 1970s, 34–14, in the first round of the play-offs. They went on to defeat the Houston Oilers in a hard-fought, controversial AFC Championship Game. Despite an up-and-down, injury-plagued season, the Steelers were heavy favorites to win their fourth Super Bowl against the wild-card NFC champion Los Angeles Rams, but the game turned into a struggle that found the Steelers trailing the Rams 13–10 at halftime and 19–17 at the end of three quarters. But the Steelers rallied behind two long passes from Terry Bradshaw to John Stallworth, the first a 73-yard bomb for a go-ahead touchdown, and a clutch interception by Jack Lambert to defeat the Rams 31–19 for their fourth Super Bowl title of the decade. Bradshaw was named the Super Bowl MVP and later shared *Sports Illustrated* Athlete of the Year honors with Willie Stargell.

FOUR DOWN, '80S TO GO

Steelers by 31–19 in Seesaw

January 21, 1980
By Vito Stellino
Pittsburgh Post-Gazette

PASADENA, CALIFORNIA—It was a coronation as well as a super Super Bowl.

The Pittsburgh Steelers, the once and future champions of pro football, were crowned again yesterday before 103,985 fans in the Rose Bowl.

For the fourth time in the last six years, they are the reigning monarchs of Pete Rozelle's kingdom.

They survived a few shaky, almost scary moments and came from behind in the final period to knock out the dogged Los Angeles Rams 31–19 in Super Bowl XIV. It followed the Steelers trademark. They not only won, but they put on a good show. In their last three Super Bowl victories, they spotted the losers an early lead and then overcame it.

"We have to stop meeting like this," Rozelle grinned on national television as he handed Art Rooney, the founding father of the Steelers, a fourth gleaming Tiffany Trophy.

After he went off camera, Rozelle said, "With the price of silver these days, that's trophy's probably worth more than what he started the franchise with in the old days."

It all began on a shoestring and $2,500 back in 1933, and now the Steelers own four Lombardi Trophies. It is fitting that they are now on the threshold of matching the ultimate in pro football: Vince Lombardi's record of five championships in a seven-year span at Green Bay in the 1960s.

They've done just about everything else. They're the first team to win four Super Bowls, the first team to win back-to-back Super Bowls twice and the second team since the modern era began after World War II to do it four times in six years.

The Steelers, who are 14–4 in playoff games and 13–2 the last six years, are now on the verge of surpassing Lombardi's Green Bay team as the best of all time.

Bradshaw Named The MVP Page 31 | Stallworth Catches Winning Pass Page 29 | Harris Scores 2 TDs Page 31 | Lambert Makes Key Interception Page 31

Pittsburgh Post-Gazette

FINAL EDITION

MONDAY, JAN. 21, 1980   20 CENTS

Four Down, '80s to Go

Carter: Boycott Olympics

By MILTON JAQUES

Steelers By 31-19 In Seesaw

By VITO STELLINO

Steelers' John Stallworth catches winning touchdown pass in fourth quarter as Rams defender Rod Perry doesn't have chance to stop him.

Revelers Pay Homage in 'Easiest' Celebration

By BOHDAN HODIAK and LINDA L. WILSON

Tito's Left Leg Is Amputated To Save Him

BELGRADE, Yugoslavia (AP)

Waldheim: 'Package' May Free U.S. Hostages

By The Associated Press

Today

Super Bonus

Airport 1980

Take My Eraser, Please

Cancer: On Camera

What's a Nice Girl

Afghan Rebels Unite

Applause: Ultralame

By DAVID GUO

January 2I. I980: the *Post-Gazette* front page after the Steelers beat the Rams for their fourth Super Bowl win.

"The record speaks for itself," Dwight White said. "I'm humble, but we keep getting better and it's reasonable to say it's the best."

Lynn Swann said, "The best team of all time? I think so."

It followed the pattern of a year that wasn't easy, a year when they survived injuries and the fact that every team was shooting at them all year long. It was a game when they made a few mistakes and weren't at their best, but they came up with the big play when they needed it.

The two biggest were a pair of touchdown strikes by Most Valuable Player Terry Bradshaw to the touchdown twins—Lynn Swann and John Stallworth. They made a showcase of their specialty in this showcase game. Swann made a leaping 47-yard touchdown catch in the end zone while Stallworth, noted for running with the ball once he catches it, hauled in one at full stride at about the 30. He dashed into the end zone in the blink of an eyelash to complete a 73-yard play in the final quarter that put the Steelers ahead for good 24–19.

A Jack Lambert interception, a 45-yard pass to Stallworth, and a 21-yard pass interference call in the end zone set up a one-yard touchdown plunge by Franco Harris that completed the scoring with less than two minutes left.

That enabled the Steelers to win by 12 and cover the 11-point spread, but it was really closer than last year's 35–31 win over Dallas when they built up a 31–17 lead midway in the final period.

It was a game in which the Rams showed they deserved to be there. There could be no jokes about them. They were beaten, but they earned a lot of respect.

They held Harris to 46 yards in 20 carries and they intercepted three Bradshaw passes. And young Vince Ferragamo almost matched Bradshaw, completing 15 of 25 passes for 212 yards while Bradshaw won the MVP honors for the second straight Super Bowl while hitting on 14 of 21 passes for 309 yards. Wendell Tyler also distinguished himself as he ran 60 yards in 17 carries, including a 39-yard run.

It was a game in which the Steelers trailed, 13–10, at the half, and there were a few anxious moments at halftime.

"It was a test of the character and the maturity of the team," White said. "We were just a little excited at halftime. We knew we couldn't keep fooling around or we could blow it."

Bradshaw described the Steelers' first-half play as "fiddling around" and added, "If we had continued the same way, we would have lost the game."

Larry Anderson, who set a Super Bowl record by returning five kicks for 162 yards, returned the second-half kickoff 37 yards to set the Steelers up at the 39.

Swann's leaping touchdown catch capped at 61-yard drive and gave the Steelers a 17–13 lead. They seemed to be in control. It seemed to be time for the Steeler defense to take over.

But the Rams refused to fold. As Ray Malavasi, the Rams coach, said, "They didn't outplay us. We ran on them. We threw on them. We just didn't get the big plays."

But they got two on the next drive. On a third-down play, Ferragamo hit on a 50-yard pass to Billy Waddy, and Lawrence McCutcheon fooled the Steelers with a 24-yard touchdown pass to Ron Smith. After Frank Corral missed the extra point, the Rams led, 19–17, with 10 minutes left in the third period.

On the Steelers' next two series, Bradshaw threw his second and third interceptions and there were a few tense moments on the Steeler sideline. The first one was a long one on third down that was almost like a short punt and really didn't hurt that much.

But on the next series, Bradshaw had a third-and-10 call on the Rams 16. With the Steelers needing a field goal to take the lead, it wasn't a time to make a mistake. But Bradshaw tried to force the ball to Stallworth. Dave Elmendorf knocked it in the air and Rod Perry intercepted it on the 5.

The Steelers forced the Rams to punt, but Ken Clark booted a 59-yarder and the Steelers took over on their own 25 with 12:59 left in the game. It was time for the Steelers to put together a long drive. When Franco Harris made only two yards on first down and Bradshaw misfired on a screen pass to Sidney Thornton, the Steelers faced a third-and-eight on their own 27. If Bradshaw didn't complete the next pass, the Steelers would have had to punt and the Rams would have had the lead and the ball in the final quarter.

It was also ominous that Swann had suffered a concussion in the third quarter and was sidelined the rest of the game.

But then came Bradshaw's 73-yard strike to Stallworth, and the Steelers were ahead for good. Stallworth had made a hook on the previous interception. This time he faked the hook and went deep and Bradshaw put it right on the money.

Noting the three interceptions, Stallworth said, "This was a typical game for us. We've had a lot of turnovers all year. But we have the type of people who come back."

The Steelers also have the type of people who win Super Bowls.

"Just awesome," is what White called it.

The Steelers are now the Super Steelers XIV. Anyone for five?

39

Pitt Defeats Georgia in the Sugar Bowl

1982

Central Catholic's Dan Marino was the most recruited Western Pennsylvania high school football player since Tony Dorsett. Growing up in Oakland in the shadow of Pitt Stadium, he decided to follow Dorsett to the University of Pittsburgh, where, after stepping into the starting quarterback position in the middle of his freshman year in 1979, he went on to break several NCAA passing records and lead Pitt to four major bowl games in his college career. His Pitt teams never won a national title, but they finished 11–1 in three consecutive seasons and were ranked second in the nation in 1980 and fourth in 1981. Marino's finest moment came in the 1982 Sugar Bowl when he defeated Georgia 24–20 and ended its hopes for a national championship with a 33-yard touchdown pass to tight end John Brown with only 33 seconds left in the game. After his career was over, the Miami Dolphins selected Marino in the first round after he was passed over by the Pittsburgh Steelers.

PANTHERS TAME DAWGS; LIONS WIN

Marino Pass Rallies Pitt

January 2, 1982
By Ron Reid
Pittsburgh Post-Gazette

NEW ORLEANS—In a march through Georgia more thrilling than any General Sherman ever knew, the 10th-ranked Pitt Panthers raised the standards of athletic drama to a new art form here last night when they beat the second-ranked Georgia Bulldogs 24–20 to win the 48th annual Sugar Bowl Classic.

And man, was this a classic! With a throat-constricting, hackle-raising finish that will be discussed in Pittsburgh saloons, Bourbon Street gin mills, and Georgia peanut mills as long as football ushers in the American New Year.

And when it was over, the hero, Dan Marino, could only say, "I threw it too far."

He didn't.

Instead, tight end John Brown raced under it in the end zone for a 33-yard touchdown reception with 35 seconds remaining that gave Pitt its dramatic victory.

Marino, named the Most Valuable Player in the game, said the play wasn't designed to go to Brown, that Pitt merely wanted to get first-down yardage on the fourth-and-5 situation.

"I never imagined they would blitz," Marino said. "I guess they thought we would run."

Brown said, "The feeling—once you realize what you did—comes as soon as you touch it."

Brown said he saw a swarm of teammates heading his way and "I wanted to run. I panicked under that pile. Claustrophobia."

The Marino-Brown combo, which struck for another score earlier in the final quarter, produced the game-winning play at the end of an 80-yard drive.

Before the game, Pitt Coach Jackie Sherrill had brewed up a two-tight-end offense as a special challenge for the Georgia defense.

It's a formation Sherrill had used not once during the 11-game regular season. And the surprise performer of the piece was Greg Christy, a 6-foot-4,

280-pound offensive tackle, who played seldom this season and who had not competed as a tight end since high school.

Long before the Panthers ever reached New Orleans, Sherrill recognized that the matchup with Vince Dooley's Bulldogs was bound to be a contest demanding something new from his usual offensive style. Christy thus started working out at tight end as soon as the Panthers hit Biloxi for a week-long training camp that preceded the team's stay here.

"What we hope to do," Sherrill said at breakfast yesterday morning, "is create a mismatch anytime they play Cover Three (a defensive alignment featuring three deep backs in the secondary). If they stay with Cover Three, the extra tight end will allow us to run or pass like we usually do. If they go to Cover Five (which deploys an extra defensive back in five-man pass coverage) we'll run quick traps and draws. This will eliminate their blitz," Sherrill said as he drew the X's and O's on a sheet of legal paper. "And we're gonna knock the Dawg-bleep out of these two defensive ends."

Georgia had hoped to use a victory over Pitt to successfully defend its 1980 national championship, but that went out the window with the Sugar Bowl and would not have mattered anyway, since top ranked Clemson completed a perfect season by beating Nebraska 22–15 in the Orange Bowl.

Dooley called Marino "truly a great, great quarterback. The tight end (Brown) made a great play, and Marino made a great play. But I don't think we can play any better. We played our hearts out to the bitter end."

Marino, who completed 26 of 41 passes for 261 yards, brought the Panthers back in the final four minutes after Georgia had taken a 20–17 advantage midway through the final quarter.

Marino, who finished with three touchdown passes in the game, hit Brown on a six-yarder early in the final quarter and connected with All-American Julius Dawkins from 30 yards in the third period.

It was the 11th victory in 12 games for the Panthers, who used a swarming defense to hold Georgia All-American tailback Herschel Walker under 100 yards rushing for the first time in 14 games.

Walker, who scored two touchdowns on runs of eight and 10 yards, was limited to only 84 yards on 25 carries as he was stalked constantly by Pitt defensive tackle Dave Puzzuoli.

Georgia, the defending national champion, got its other TD on a six-yard pass from Buck Belue to Clarence Kay with 8:31 left in game. The Bulldogs finished with a 10–2 record.

Pitt's other score came in the second quarter, a 41-yard field goal by Snuffy Everett.

Georgia appeared to have the victory in hand when Pitt failed on a fourth-down fake punt gamble at midfield with only 5:29 left to play, but the Bulldogs failed to move and were forced to punt with Pitt taking over at its 20 with 3:46 remaining.

Marino had an 18-yard pass to halfback Bryan Thomas and an eight-yard run in the game-winning drive.

The winning touchdown came on a pass right down the middle as Brown made the catch in the end zone without breaking stride.

Georgia's go-ahead march earlier in the quarter featured a 23-yard scamper by Belue and a 24-yard run by Walker on which he ran over All-American linebacker Sal Sunseri.

Walker also turned in a tackle-breaking effort to set up Georgia's first touchdown when he hauled in a short pass at the Pitt 40 and completed a 31-yard run to the 15 on which he broke through four defenders.

Georgia's first score came on a 51-yard drive after Clarence Kay recovered Tom Flynn's fumble on a punt return.

The Bulldogs also capitalized on a fumble recovery for their second touchdown when Eddie Weaver recovered a fumbled pitch-out by Thomas at the Pitt 10.

Marino connected on five of six short passes for 16 yards in the drive that ended with Everett's field goal and cut Georgia's halftime lead to 7–3.

40

Willie Stargell Hits Pirates' Record 475th Home Run

1982

Willie Stargell was the greatest left-handed slugger in Pirates history, but he had the misfortune of playing the first half of his career in spacious Forbes Field. He broke Dale Long's single-season home run record of 27 for a left-handed hitter when he hit 33 home runs in 1966, but in his first nine seasons, from 1962 to 1970, he never topped his 1966 home-run total. In 1971, his first full season in the friendlier confines of Three Rivers Stadium, he hit 48 home runs and followed that total with 44 home runs in 1973. In 1979, at the age of 39 and in the twilight of his career, Stargell hit 32 home runs on his way to the co-MVP award. He was also named the MVP of the NLCS and the World Series that year. He struggled with injuries over the next few season, but, in 1982, he hit his 475th and last home run off Tom Hulme of the Cincinnati Reds and tied Stan Musial for 14th place on the all-time home run list.

STARGELL HR WINS FOR PIRATES, 3–2

Captain Ties Musial for 14th Place

July 22, 1982
By Charley Feeney
Pittsburgh Post-Gazette

CINCINNATI—It was the Pops Stargell Show last night as he said farewell to Riverfront Stadium, where the Pirates defeated the Cincinnati Reds 3–2 before 16,543 fans.

When Stargell crashed a tie-breaking pinch home run off Tom Hume in the eighth inning, many of the fans treated him like a hometown hero. They stood and cheered, and when the game was over and Stargell was being interviewed on radio by Jim Rooker in the visitors' dugout, about 300 fans stood near the box seats, shouting good luck remarks to the 41-year-old veteran who plans to retire at the end of the season.

This was Willie's last hurrah in Cincinnati, where in the 1979 playoffs he beat Hume with a three-run homer.

Last night's circuit was career No. 475 for Stargell, tying him for 14th place with Stan Musial on the all-time list.

"Musial?" Stargell said. "I never thought I'd ever be in his company. He was one of my idols when I was growing up and now I know him. What a great guy."

As Stargell spoke to a group of writers on the field following his radio interview, one fan shouted, "Thanks for a great 21 years, Willie."

"It's heartwarming hearing something like that," said Stargell, who joined the Pirates in 1962 and who in his last year is playing out a wonderful tune as a pinch hitter.

His pinch circuit last night tied a Pirate club record held by four others who also hit three pinch homers in one season. Stargell has almost a half a season left to break that mark.

The drama of Stargell's home run overshadowed some big performances by several Buccos.

Larry McWilliams, the bargain find from Atlanta, won his fourth game

Fan favorite Willie Stargell tips his hat to an appreciative Pittsburgh crowd. (Marlene Karas/ *Post-Gazette*)

as a Buc. McWilliams gave up a two-run homer to Paul Householder in the fourth inning. It wiped out a 1–0 Buc lead that was accounted for by Dale Berra, who homered in the third inning off Bob Shirley.

Tony Pena's RBI double high off the left field wall in the seventh tied the game, and Russ Nixon, the new Cincinnati manager who replaced John McNamara earlier in the day, made his first pitching move.

He lifted Shirley for a pinch-hitter in the bottom of the seventh and Hume came on in the eighth.

After Berra flied out to open the eighth, Stargell batted for McWilliams. On July 8, Stargell hit a two-run homer off Hume that sparked a five-run ninth-inning rally. This time, Stargell lined over the right field wall and as he trotted around the bases, many of the Cincinnati fans saluted him with cheers.

For the sixth straight game, Kent Tekulve relieved, and after a routine one-two-three eighth, Tekulve needed some breaks in the ninth.

"I didn't exactly fool them in the ninth," said Tekulve, who told Chuck Tanner before the start of the inning that he was tired.

Cesar Cedeno led off the ninth with a wicked liner toward the mound. Tekulve got his glove on the ball and it rolled slowly toward second base.

Berra charged, barehanded the ball, and flipped it to Jason Thompson to retire Cedeno by a half step. Next came Dan Driessen. He hit another line drive. It went directly at Dave Parker in right field. Then Householder took his cuts. Nothing big there. He hit a high pop to Omar Moreno in center.

Tekulve, in his last six appearances, has worked 7⅔ innings. Twice he asked to pitch because had had three days off during the break for the All-Star Game.

When he started in the ninth last night, Enrique Romo and Randy Niemann were warming up in the bullpen.

"If Teke had gotten in trouble, I was going to go to the pen," said Tanner, who many times sinks or swims in the ninth with his bullpen ace.

The four Pirates, beside Stargell, who have hit three pinch home runs are Hamilton Hyatt, Bob Skinner, Dick Stuart, and Jose Pagan.

If the baseball script goes Hollywood, Stargell is sure to become the only Pirate to hit four pinch homers in one season.

41

Pitt's Roger Kingdom Wins Olympic Gold Medal in the 110-Meter High Hurdles

1984

In the 1984 Olympic games held in Los Angeles, Georgia-born Roger Kingdom became the first Pitt athlete to win a gold medal since John Woodruff at the 1936 Berlin Olympics. Running in the 110-meter hurdles, Kingdom, who thought, at first, he'd finished second in the race, barely nipped his heavily favored teammate Greg Foster at the finish line. Four years later, in the 1988 Seoul Olympics, a heavily favored Roger Kingdom easily won his second consecutive gold medal in the 110-meters and set a world record in the event. During his brilliant career, Kingdom won five United States Outdoor Championships, two gold medals at the Pan-Am Games, and a World Cup gold medal, He was ranked No. 1 at his event for five different years in a span from 1984 to 1990. After his career was over, he was inducted into the National Track and Field Hall of Fame in 2005.

PITT'S KINGDOM WINS GOLD

August 7, 1984
By Tom McMillan
Pittsburgh Post-Gazette

LOS ANGELES—The feeling, at first, was a peculiar one. He did not know. Roger Kingdom crossed the finish line in the Olympic 110-meter hurdles last night and looked up, puzzled. "I thought," he said, "I came in second."

So he watched the replay on a screen high above the Los Angeles Memorial Coliseum, and what he saw was R. Kingdom of Vienna, Georgia, slicing himself a little piece of Olympic history. Kingdom, the University of Pittsburgh student, had laser-beamed his way past Greg Foster to win the Olympic gold medal in an astounding international upset. His time was 13.20 seconds, an Olympic record.

"I knew I surged at the fourth hurdle, I knew I was coming," Kingdom said later in the press tent. "But I didn't know what place I got when I crossed the finish line. This guy's [Foster] been running hurdles for years, and he's ranked No. 1 in the world. I just didn't feel I overtook him at the line."

But he stood there and watched the replay, and he hoped a lot, and he saw his future flash before him. He watched the runner in lane eight arrive three-hundredths of a second before the runner in lane one, and he knew, only then, that this gold medal was for him.

"The feeling?" Roger Kingdom said 45 minutes later. "I…I can't explain it."

Foster, the defending world champion and overwhelming gold medal favorite, crossed second in 13.23—also under the 12-year-old Olympic record of 13.24, set by Rod Milburn in the Munich Games. Finland's Arto Bryggare won the bronze in 13.40 and was followed by Mark McKoy of Canada (13.45) and Tonie Campbell of the U.S. (13.55).

Foster—"I would've liked the gold, but I'm happy with the silver"—blamed his loss on a false start the officials failed to notice.

He said it was his false start, and that he eased up momentarily, costing him the race.

"I think I [false started]," Foster said, "but the starter didn't recall the race. I eased up and I shouldn't have. That's my fault."

1984 Olympic gold medalist Roger Kingdom enters Pitt Stadium at halftime of the Pitt-Oklahoma game. (John Kaplan/*Post-Gazette*)

Bob Kersee, Foster's coach, observed the hesitation from the stands and said, "I died." But it was Kersee who bolted into the interview tent to hug Kingdom, to slap his chest. And Foster, denied the anticipated gold, joined him in a victory lap around the Coliseum track.

"I didn't see anything," Kingdom said of the false-start flap, "but Greg was in lane one and I was in lane eight. I didn't see him until the sixth hurdle."

Kingdom, 21, became Pitt's first Olympic medalist since Herb Douglas long-jumped his way to a bronze in 1948, and his gold medal caps one of the more dramatic nobody-to-somebody ascents of these Games. Kingdom had gone to Pitt on a football scholarship, and was hurdling anonymity as recently as 18 months ago. In January 1983, the Millrose Games, a prestigious indoor meet held at Madison Square Garden, turned down his application.

Kingdom, a little-used defensive back in his first two years at Pitt, offered his first gold-metal hint when he surprisingly won the NCAA hurdles championship in 1983, defeating Willie Gault of the University of Tennessee. He floundered in The Athletics Congress national championships that year, finishing seventh, but he resurfaced in the Pan-American Games when Foster and Gault declined to participate. In his first international competition, Kingdom won the Pan-Am gold in 13.44.

He took a football redshirt last fall to concentrate on Olympic preparations, then won an NCAA indoor hurdles championship in 1984. He asked for another redshirt for the outdoor track season, not only for Olympian reasons, but also because of a question about his academic eligibility.

Kingdom finished an expected third at the U.S. Olympic trials, running third to Foster and Campbell in a personal-best 13.36. He lowered that to 13.32 shortly after the trials, then ripped off a wind-aided 13.00 in an Olympic preparatory meet. Although the time was unofficial because of a 2.6 mile-an-hour wind, Kingdom had dipped within seven-hundredths of a second of Renaldo Nehemiah's world record of 12.93.

"When I ran the 13-flat," he said yesterday, "it gave me a lot of confidence that I'd do well in the Olympics." But he had been considered the bronze medal favorite, behind Foster and Campbell, because he was a mediocre technician, a runner who banged many hurdles.

"He's come a long way…a long way," Kersee said. "He used to hit hurdles, used to run flat-footed. He doesn't do that anymore. He's a great hurdler."

Still, Kingdom had to overcome a slightly strained hamstring, suffered in a workout less than two weeks before. He missed six days of practice, then returned for three days before Sunday's preliminary round. He admitted looking "sluggish" while qualifying in 13.53.

But Kingdom was outstanding in the finals last night, surging at the fourth hurdle, catching Foster near the ninth and then outrunning him to the electronic tape. His time of 13.20 is the second fastest in the world this year—behind the 13.19 Foster ran at the Olympic trials—and the fourth fastest of all time. Foster called him the "heir apparent." Said Kersee, "Roger has a great future.

Whether the future will include football or track at Pitt is unclear at the moment. "I'm definitely coming back to school," said Kingdom, who is expected to tour Europe with the U.S. Olympic team this month, "but I can't really comment. I still might play football. It's definitely a possibility."

Elbert Kennedy, Kingdom's coach with the New Image Track Club, watched him race on television back home in Pittsburgh and gave him a glowing review.

"He looked real good," Kennedy said. "The things we talked about last week, he did. It was just like we planned. I told him not to take those little bitty steps."

Kennedy, who also coaches the Pitt women's team and who convinced Kingdom to take time off from intercollegiate meets to prepare for the Olympics, said he wasn't surprised by Kingdom's performance.

"He got pretty sharp last week when he ran the 13-flat wind-aided," Kennedy said. "I told him just to relax after that. I didn't want anything negative to get in his mind."

Kennedy's own thoughts were increasingly positive as he watched the race develop.

"When Tonie jumped, I knew he wasn't going to get it," he said, referring to Campbell. "I knew Greg was going to fold if anybody was with him after the seventh hurdle. I knew nobody could stay with Roger between the hurdles."

And just in case, he did more than think positive thoughts. "I'm praying all the way," the coach said.

42

Penguins Win Two Consecutive Stanley Cups

1991 and 1992

When the National Hockey League expanded in 1966 from its original six teams to 12, the league awarded one of its new franchises to Pittsburgh. Dubbed the Penguins, the Pittsburgh franchise began play in the 1967–1968 NHL hockey season. The team made the playoffs for the first time in 1970 and for seven out of eight seasons from 1975–1982. After faltering and finishing with the worst record in hockey in 1984, the Penguins drafted Mario Lemieux with the first overall pick. In took four years for the team to return to the playoffs, but, led by Lemieux's brilliant play, the Penguins became a Stanley Cup contender. In 1991, after a late-season trade brought Ron Francis and Ulf Samuelsson to the team, the Penguins went on to the playoff finals and defeated the Minnesota North Stars in six games to win the franchise's first Stanley Cup. Despite the tragic loss of the team's coach, Bob Johnson, the Penguins won their second Stanley Cup a year later under interim coach Scotty Bowman with a sweep of the Chicago Blackhawks in the finals. The only problem for jubilant Pittsburgh hockey fans was that, because of a strike, there was no newspaper coverage of the Penguins victory.

CHAMPIONS

Penguins Claim Stanley Cup

May 27, 1991
By Tom McMillan
Pittsburgh Post-Gazette

In a light-hearted moment the day before the game, someone asked Mario Lemieux if lifting the Stanley Cup would put undue strain on his chronically tender back.

Lemieux giggled.

"No problem," the Penguins captain said.

And now we have the proof.

On a night of snapshot memories frozen into Pittsburgh sports lore, Lemieux and his indomitable teammates scaled the National Hockey League's biggest, steepest mountain. Behind Lemieux's four points, Joe Mullen's two goals, and Tom Barrasso's 39 saves, the Penguins drubbed the Minnesota North Stars 8–0 Saturday at the Met Center to win the best-of-seven final series, four games to two. Then they carried the cup around the rink. Forever

"To see that, to feel that, and to pick up the Cup—to pick it up—that's the greatest feeling I've ever had," a delirious Phil Bourque was saying. "Unbelievable. I can't think of anything I'd rather do in life than skate around with the Cup over my head."

Hoisting the hallowed hockey silverware is always a special experience because of the history involved, the names of the players engraved on the sides—great players from the greatest teams of all time. The Montreal Canadiens. The Boston Bruins. The Edmonton Oilers.

But it meant even more to this team, to this town, at this moment, because it capped a season of firsts in the 24-year-history of the long-suffering Penguins franchise—the first division title; the first conference championship; the first finals appearance; the first Cup.

"And, boy, I'm so proud right now for the city of Pittsburgh," said Troy Loney, a Pittsburgh kind of guy from Bow Island, Alberta, who's been with the organization since 1982. "It's been a 20-year struggle for our fans, but they stuck with us. This is the reward. For all of us."

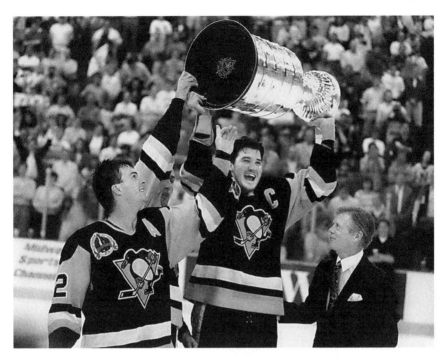

Bob Errey (left) watches Mario Lemieux hoist the Stanley Cup after the Penguins' victory over the Minnesota North Stars. (Darrell Sapp/*Post-Gazette*)

Not that it was ever easy—at least not until the last two periods Saturday, when the Penguins' grit and talent and sense of destiny overwhelmed the helpless Stars. It was a long, arduous battle to get to that final night, that clinching victory. A long way from October to 8–0.

Think of it. They began the season without Lemieux, their symbolic leader and best player, felled for 50 games by a back infection. They began it with a new coach, Bob Johnson, who had to prod and cajole and badger them into playing his system—into playing team defense.

They went through a 2–9–1 skid in November and December. They found a rich chemistry despite innumerable roster changes. Craig Patrick, the low-key general manager, once made three trades in 11 days in the weeks leading up to Christmas. No matter. They pulled through.

But even Johnson's hope was dimming in early March, when they wobbled home from a 0–4–1 road trip, having been blitzed for 28 goals in five games. So Patrick—seizing the moment—made the most monumental trade in club history on March 4, on the eve of the trading deadline. He shipped John Cullen, Zarley Zalapski, and Jeff Parker to Hartford for Ron Francis, Ulf Samuelsson, and Grant Jennings.

"But that's the thing about Craig," Johnson was saying in a corner of the dressing room late Saturday. "He's always looking to help the club. He's not afraid to make deals."

Fueled by more character and defense than ever before, the Penguins went on a 9–2–1 roll to overtake the New York Rangers for first place in the Patrick Division—named for Patrick's grandfather Lester. They neared the regular season title with a suffocating 3–1 win at the Philadelphia Spectrum, their traditional den of horrors. They clinched it a night later by bonking Detroit 7–4 at Joe Louis Arena.

Then came the playoffs.

"And you could just feel the thing building," Bryan Trottier said.

The thing built through bouts with adversity in every round. The Penguins lost the first game of the each of their four playoff series—and the first two games against Boston. They trailed, 3–2, heading to Game 6 of the division semifinals at New Jersey.

They survived.

Frank Pietrangelo and "The Save" bailed them out. Jim Paek, a rookie defenseman who spent most of the year with the Canadian national team, bailed them out. The list of unsung heroes runs off the page—Randy Gilhen, Paul Stanton, Bob Errey, Jay Caufield.

"We had adversity every step of the way, the injuries and all, falling behind, but that just made our team stronger," Johnson said. "We were better in Washington than we were in Jersey. We were better in Boston than we were in Washington."

They were best of all in the end against Minnesota. Paired with one of the most charming Cinderella teams of recent vintage, the Penguins lost Game 1 on home ice, lost Game 3 without Lemieux (back spasms)—and never blinked.

Kevin Stevens, their emerging vocal leader, wouldn't let them. Samuelsson wouldn't let them. Barrasso wouldn't let them.

The North Stars feasted on Chicago, St. Louis, and Edmonton in earlier rounds by jumping to sudden leads, dominating the first period. But the Penguins crushed them by a combined 10–2 in the opening periods of Games 4, 5, and 6.

They gutted out a 5–3 victory win at the Met Center in Game 4, tying the series at two games apiece, then returned home for a game five love fest with their fans. Mark Recchi, the team MVP in the regular season, broke a four-game drought by exploding for two goals in the first period, staking the Penguins to a quick 4–0 lead. They won it 6–4 to snatch a 3–2 series edge.

Leading the series 3–2 they rumbled back to Minnesota Saturday on the brink of the Cup, and it was strange scene in the dressing room after the morning skate. Something Loney—who's been around—had never sensed before.

"The guys were so nervous, so ready, so keyed up that it was scary," he said. "I could see we were going to win it. That we were going to win the Cup. You could feel it."

They skated out with icy stares and thumping hearts and took care of business early. The defense-minded Samuelsson got them started with a power-play goal at the two-minute mark, and the snowball rolled down the hill from there.

Lemieux scored a short-handed goal for the highlights film at 12:19 and Mullen added another before the end of the first period to make it 3–0. Then Errey, Francis and Mullen again in the middle period. Then Paek ("don't wake me up") and Larry Murphy in the third.

Eight-nothing. The largest margin for a final series game in this century. And when the league officials rolled out the Cup and handed it to Lemieux, the Penguins went properly—and indescribably—bonkers.

The celebration lasted long into the night, with wives and parents and children and office workers dancing in the dressing room, with everyone hugging, with players themselves taking photos of the big silver mug.

Even Paul Coffey, who's been here before—who's won four Cups in his storybook career—pulled out an instamatic and snapped away.

"It never gets old, this feeling," Coffey said. "Never. Never."

Meanwhile, Johnson, the 60-year-old coach who won it for the first time, stood back and crossed his arms and bounced on his toes and drank it all in.

"This will mean more to them in July than it does now, and it will mean more in five years than it does in July," he said.

"Think of it. Their names are on the Cup. They're enshrined forever."

43

Korie Hlede Becomes the First Duquesne Basketball Player to Score 2,000 Points

1997

Beginning with Paul Birch and Moe Becker in the 1930s, Duquesne has had a tradition of All-American basketball players, including Chuck Cooper, Dick Ricketts, Si Green, Willie Somerset, and Norm Nixon. But Korie Hlede was the first and only Duquesne player, male or female, to score more than 2,000 points in a career. Born in Zagreb, Croatia, the 5'9" Hlede ended her career at Duquesne with 2,631 points. She was the 1995 Atlantic 10 Freshman of the Year and the 1996 and 1998

Player of the Year. She holds school career records in scoring, assists, and steals and set the single game scoring record with 42 points against Dayton in her senior year. Korie was picked by the Detroit Storm in the first round of the 1998 WNBA draft and finished second in voting for the Rookie of the Year. After a successful professional career, she began coaching at the professional and collegiate level. Hlede is the only female athlete in Duquesne history to have her number retired.

MAKING HISTORY AT DUQUESNE

Hlede First Player to Surpass 2,000

December 8, 1997
By Marino Parascenzo
Pittsburgh Post-Gazette

Maybe this time it would have been more blessed to get than to give.

If Korie Hlede was thinking about that scoring milestone, it didn't show in the open shots she passed up early in the game to feed her teammates. And later, when the Lady Dukes were in trouble and finally started going to her, it was too little and too late.

Hlede got her 2,000th point and them some, with a game-high 26 points, but the San Diego State Aztecs (2–3) cashed in a flurry of errors, pounded the boards, and ended the Lady Dukes' five-game winning streak, 64–59, at the Palumbo Center yesterday.

Hlede, a 5-foot-9 senior, now has 2,020 career points.

"In light of the loss, it doesn't mean much," Hlede said. "But it is an achievement, and I'm happy."

Hlede became the first Duquesne player, man or woman, to reach 2,000 career points with 9:46 to play in the first half on a driving layup. It gave her point No. 2,000 and an 18–13 Duquesne lead.

Moments later, at the next timeout, the achievement was announced to a small but appreciative crowd.

Hlede was in the spotlight all day. The view of her play perhaps depended on your seat.

Aztecs Coach Barb Smith said it was the defense she put on Hlede that produced the victory.

"Our game plan was to take (Hlede) out of her game early, and that worked," Smith said.

In the man-to-man defense, it was Shaneya Harris, a 5–11 senior, who drew Hlede.

"Our best defensive player—and also a little taller," Smith said.

Duquesne Dukes' Korie Hlede (25) goes up for her 2000ᵗʰ career point during the first half against San Diego State. (Joyce Mendelsohn/*Post-Gazette*)

"Going into the game, we knew we had to force her to her right," Harris said. "On video, we saw she likes to fake you right, then go to her left. So I forced her to the right."

It worked. Hlede got only 8 of her 26 points in the first half. She hit her first shot, shaking Harris for a 15-footer and a 2–2 tie in the first minute.

Moments later, Hlede missed a driving layup. Then she got to the left wing with no trouble twice, but missed two 3-pointers. Right after she scored her 2,000ᵗʰ point, Hlede passed up a chance for two more, passing instead to Jaime Vander Zanden under the basket. It didn't pay off.

Hlede passed up at least six open shots in the first half and came up with four of her eight assists. Harris remained on Hlede in the second half, but Hlede scored 16 points.

Duquesne trailed 28–26 at the half, then broke down under defensive pressure.

Krista Thomas misfired on two passes and missed catching one, and San Diego converted them into seven points.

Olivia DeCamilli, who led the Aztecs with 22 points, made a layup to complete an 11–2 run for a 39–28 lead with 16 minutes to play.

Before long, Duquesne coach Dan Durkin pulled point guard Sherri Hannan, and her backup, Gina Naccarato, and said give the ball to Hlede.

"We were a little stagnant," Durkin said. "I was trying to get something going."

Hlede was playing point guard for the first time this year, and from that moment on, the Lady Dukes started crawling back into the game.

Hlede hit a 15-footer, swiped the ball and made a layup, hit a 3-pointer, then two free throws. LynnDee Howell added two quick 6-footers, and Thomas hit a 12-footer to tie the score, 57–57, with 2:10 left.

The Lady Dukes could not push ahead. Courtney Bale's layup put San Diego on top at 1:52, and after Howell's two free throws tied it again, the Aztecs finished the game with five free throws for the 64–59 final.

It was enough to spoil Korie Hlede's day. And she wouldn't be celebrating the record.

"We have finals," she said.

44

Lightweight Paul Spadafora Wins 32nd Consecutive Fight in Title Defense

2000

McKees Rocks' Paul Spadafora is not the first boxing champion to grow up on Pittsburgh's mean streets, but his life outside the ring may be the most troubling of all of Pittsburgh's great fighters. After winning 75 of 80 amateur bouts, the southpaw Spadafora turned professional in 1995 and fought his way to the International Boxing Federation Lightweight Title in 1999. He went on to defend his IBF title eight times, including a controversial match against Billy Irwin in Pittsburgh, and had an unblemished record until he fought to a draw against WBA Lightweight champion Leonard Dorin in early 2003. After the fight Spadafora announced he was moving up to the Junior Welterweight Division, but a few months later he was arrested and charged with shooting his pregnant girlfriend. In early 2005 he was sentenced to 21 to 60 months for the shooting. After serving 13 months, Spadafora was released from prison but, after attempting a boxing comeback, had to return after being charged with a parole violation. When the charge was dropped, he was released and resumed his comeback and his undefeated career.

BACK IN STYLE

Spadafora's Form Returns as He Scores Unanimous Decision

December 17, 2000
By Chuck Finder
Pittsburgh Post-Gazette

Last night, Paul Spadafora picked up his hands and turned back the hands of time. He restored his style to the defensive-posture fighter last seen in August 1999, when he first won the International Boxing Federation light-weight title, and last December, when he first successfully defended his belt. He counterpunched, eluded, survived, hoisted his arms in a 32nd consecutive victory salute.

Now that he is back, now that he has thumped mandatory challenger Billy Irwin, the McKees Rocks boxer wants to raise not only his hands but his level of competition.

"I want to come back and fight the best," Spadafora said after winning nine of the 12 rounds at the David L. Lawrence Convention Center for a unanimous decision against the Niagara Falls, Ontario, puncher who hardly punched.

"I want to fight the good fighters like [Floyd] Mayweather, [Diego] Corrales, [Angel] Manfreddy, Arturo Gatti. I just want to fight the best fighters to see if I am the real deal…and I think I am.

"I'm 32–0. It's time to let me get a chance. I can fight with those guys. I want to prove it."

Funny he should mention Gatti. Like that fighter in a ballyhooed bout earlier this year, HBO's scale showed

Spadafora was a fight-night bloated 153 pounds, some 18 higher than his weigh-in the day before. And, more important, that was 12½ pounds more than the 140½ that he measured at 8:30 yesterday morning, in the official weigh-in by Pennsylvania State Athletic Commissioner Greg Sirb.

"That was on an official scale," an angry Sirb said while the HBO "KO Nation" announcers were criticizing the champion's purported weight gain. "Not on a bathroom scale like HBO. What they said is dead wrong. That's terrible journalism."

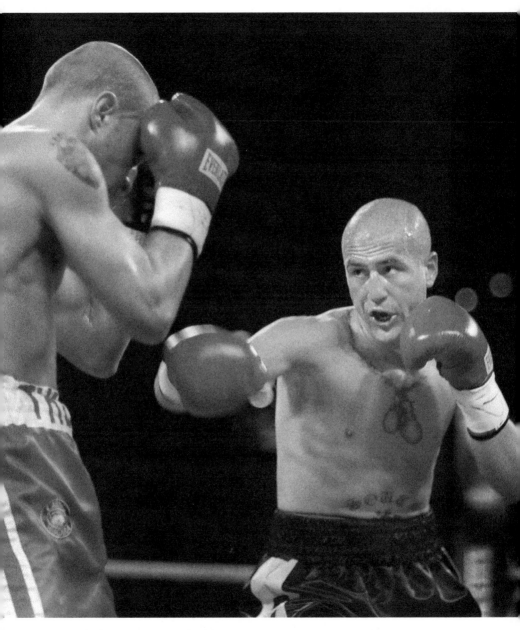

Billy Irwin (left) and Pittsburgh's Paul Spadafora exchange punches in the second round of their IBF lightweight title bout. (Gabor Degre/*Post-Gazette*)

Spadafora claimed the cable network weighed him when he was in his pregame warmup togs, replete with two pair of sweatpants and heavy hiking boots. For a counter puncher who doesn't possess knockout power, excess girth doesn't mean much, whether it is 5½ pounds or more than a dozen.

"It didn't matter," said Irwin (34–4), who lost for the first time after 11 consecutive knockouts, and rarely showed his punching power yesterday for the "KO Nation" audience and the 5,500 witnesses inside the Convention Center. "He didn't punch hard at all. He's just a very good boxer. That's all it was, a style fight.

"If he fights any boxer with any kind of a punch, [the opponent] will have no problem, because he has no punch at all."

Spadafora came out firing from the get-go. He initiated the action, while Irwin stayed at a distance—a surprising move, considering his view of Spadafora's absence of power. Yet early on, Irwin found that he would have trouble finding Spadafora without radar. Irwin punched. Spadafora ducked, bobbed, weaved. The knockout puncher's gloves missed.

When the bout reached the one-quarter pole, after the fourth round, Spadafora had landed more than twice as many punches as Irwin. In fact, he landed more power punches by HBO's count, seven to five.

The difference only got more pronounced as the fight progressed into the early evening.

"I felt like he made me miss," Irwin said. "He made me look wild and sloppy.

"No excuses. I got out-stroked."

In the fifth, while a brawl erupted in the Convention Center seats, Irwin landed his match high of eight power punches. No matter, for Spadafora again landed more than twice as many: 17 of 25 power-punch attempts.

Irwin did connect in the third round, a left just underneath Spadafora's eye that dazed the champ and left a welt. In the 11th, Spadafora got a point deducted by referee Rick Steigerwald of the North Side for a low blow. Still, Irwin didn't seem to win a second round until the seventh, at the earliest. He didn't fully unleash his arsenal until the 12th and final round.

Promoter Mike Acri considered it a near shutout, though the judges scored in Spadafora's favor, 117–110, 118–109, and 116–101.

Whatever the score, whatever the outcome, this fighter in the black-and-gold trunks looked more like the one who wrested the IBF lightweight belt from Israel "Pito" Cardona and defended first against Renato Cornett, 53 weeks ago in this same Convention Center. He admitted afterward that he should have been counted out, a knockout victim, against Victoriano Damien Sosa last March in New York. He admitted that weight problems—he called consumption his "addiction…my family, we're all Italian, we love to eat"—played a role in his lackluster performance against Mike Griffith on HBO's "KO Nation" in May.

With his waistline battle supposedly conquered with the help from a new nutritionist, his camp stability restored by the addition of longtime trainer Tom Yankello to the mix with Jesse Reid, the McKees Rocks boxer believes he has everything in place.

Including the Spadafora style that initially got him this title: defensive boxing, bobbing, weaving, counter-punching, outlasting opponents.

He unfurled punch counts in the 60s through the opening eight rounds, thrice going into the 70s, and dropped only into the mid-50s by fight's end. As he jumped on the turnbuckles to address his hometown crowd, he pronounced that he could go another 12 rounds. He may get that wish come early spring, against a more nationally known fighter such as Manfreddy—whose wife watched the fight and wished Spadafora well beforehand—or the victor of an upcoming Mayweather-Corrales match.

"I feel I'm back," said Spadafora, who took home around a $75,000 payday and Irwin less than one-third of that. "I'm way more mature. As long as I keep my style and do the right things, if I do that I'll be able to get out of here with a lot of money, all my brains…and I'll be able to say I beat the best."

45

Beaver Falls Defeats Aliquippa in WPIAL Championship Thriller

2005

The Western Pennsylvania area has produced many of the greatest athletes in modern sports history. Over the years, Aliquippa and Beaver Falls have been among the most successful programs in Western Pennsylvania sports history. In the 2005 WPIAL basketball championship final, the two schools played in what many regard as the greatest game in WPIAL history. Winners of numerous WPIAL titles and bitter rivals, the schools battled throughout regulation time until Beaver Falls' All-Stater Lance Jeter sent the game into overtime with a desperation three-point shot at the buzzer. Three overtimes later, Lance Jeter made the winning basket in a 79–78 Beaver Falls victory. One of the best all-around athletes in WPIAL history, Jeter accepted a football scholarship at the University of Cincinnati. He eventually transferred to Nebraska where he became a starter on the school's basketball team in the 2010–2011 season.

BEAVER FALLS WINS IN 3 OTS

Last-Second 3-Pointer Decides Boys' AA Thriller

February 27, 2005
By Terry Shields
Pittsburgh Post-Gazette

When it comes to any Aliquippa–Beaver Falls athletic competition, from football to tiddlywinks, familiarity breeds intensity, heart-pounding excitement and, of course that old standby, contempt.

And so it was again last night before a packed house at the Palumbo Center as these two longtime Beaver County rivals battled with the WPIAL Class AA boys' basketball title on the line.

The latest rendition of this passion play yielded one of the greatest WPIAL championship games in history.

Beaver Falls (23–3) pulled out a 79–78 thriller in triple overtime as Lance Jeter banked in a 3-pointer from about 30 feet out to win it.

For Jeter, a 6-foot-3 junior guard who finished with 37 points, it was the final exclamation point on a night of heroics.

"It's just Lance," Beaver Falls coach Doug Biega said after the pulsating victory. "God blesses certain people with tremendous athletic ability and he's one of them.

"If it had been anyone else throwing up that shot, I probably would have just gotten up and walked over to the Aliquippa bench to congratulate Marvin [Emerson, the Quips coach]. But because it was Lance, I figured it had a chance."

For his part, Jeter was humbled by the turn of events.

"I guess I'm lucky," he said, referring to the deciding shot. "I just threw it up there."

Yep, he just threw it up there after dribbling up the floor after Sjavante Gilliam's apparent winning lay-in with about five seconds showing on the clock, taking a quick peek at the clock then wedging his body between two Aliquippa defenders to launch the game's final dagger.

Jeter turned in an unbelievable performance on a night of outstanding efforts on both sides. He was 13 of 16 from the field, including 4 of 6 from three-point range. He was 7 of 10 from the free-throw line and had five rebounds.

Beaver Falls' Lance Jeter shoots the winning basket with one second left in triple OT to beat Aliquippa. (Lake Fong/*Post-Gazette*)

Oh yeah, and he made another three-pointer as the buzzer sounded at the end of regulation to send the game into the first overtime.

As one might expect in a game that was so closely and hotly contested, there was plenty of glory for both sides to share. Aliquippa's Herb Pope, a 6-foot-10 sophomore, scored 24 points, snared 14 rebounds and had 3 blocked shots before fouling out with 1:46 left in the second overtime.

He was joined on the bench by another Quips standout, 6-3 sophomore forward Mark Lay, who scored 20 points and grabbed eight rebounds before fouling out in the third overtime. Included among his points was a driving baseline layup with less than a second remaining in the first overtime to force the second overtime.

For Beaver Falls it was its seventh WPIAL title, but its first in Class AA (the previous six were Class AAA or its equivalent), the most recent in 1994.

It also was the rubber match of the season series between the Section 2-AA co-champions. Beaver Falls won the first meeting on its home court 80–51, but the Quips (21–7) exacted some revenge on their court, 71–64. But this one topped those for excitement.

"I can't remember being part of a game nearly this exciting," Emerson said. "No game was even close. "What are you going to do? Lance comes up and hits the clutch shots. What can you say? I guess you just have to give the credit to Lance."

The game was tight throughout. The largest lead by either team was a seven-point spread by Beaver Falls, 12–5 in the first quarter.

The Quips had a six-point edge in the final minute of regulation, but that was negated by two three-point shots from Beaver Falls, one by Dom Henderson and then Jeter's at the buzzer.

Beaver Falls will meet Washington in the first round of the PIAA tournament; Aliquippa will face Farrell.

The Tigers ruined Aliquippa's bid for its third consecutive WPIAL crown, but Biega wasn't about to gloat.

"Before I left for the game, I told my wife, 'This is like the Yankees and the Red Sox.' And the Quips are the Yankees, they always seem to win the big one.

"I figured it was going to be decided in dramatic fashion, but not like this. It doesn't get any better than this."

Well, not unless the two meet again in the PIAA western regional final.

46

Steelers Super Bowl Victory over the Seattle Seahawks

2006

After the Steelers won their fourth Super Bowl, the rallying cry in Pittsburgh was "one for the thumb," but their fans would have to wait nearly thirty years before the Steelers won a fifth Super Bowl. After losing Super Bowl XXX to the Dallas Cowboys in 1995, the Steelers returned to the Super Bowl a decade later in 2006 after a remarkable late regular season and playoff rally. To make it into the playoffs, the Steelers, at 6–6, had to win their last four games. In the playoffs as a wild card, they had to play on the road and defeat the Bengals, Colts, and Broncos, After winning seven games in a row, including a thriller over Peyton Manning's Indianapolis Colts, the Steelers garnered a well-earned trip to the Super Bowl and defeated the Seattle Seahawks in Detroit, the hometown of retiring Steelers great, Jerome Bettis. After the victory, Hines Ward became the second wide receiver in Steelers history to win the Super Bowl Most Valuable Player award. A year later, Bill Cowher followed Bettis by stepping down as head coach.

SUPER BOWL XL: STEELERS 21, SEAHAWKS 10

The Bus Says His Run Stops Here

February 6, 2006
By Robert Dvorchak
Pittsburgh Post-Gazette

Some will call it one for the thumb, but it was truly one for the ages.

No team had ever won three playoff games on the road and then won a Super Bowl, but the Steelers last night completed a magical ride with a 21–10 victory over the Seahawks, igniting celebrations throughout the far-flung Steeler Nation.

Their Super Bowl triumph was the team's first in 26 years and the fifth in franchise history, putting the Steelers in company with Dallas and San Francisco with five Super Bowl wins.

"We were proud of the team of the '70s, but we have our own little niche right now," said coach Bill Cowher, who won his first title in 14 years and is the first coach other than Chuck Noll to bring home a championship. "It's a special team."

Although the Super Bowl is supposed to be a neutral site, the week and the game were dominated by towel-twirling Steelers fans who made the game and the on-field trophy presentation a Pittsburgh event.

The championship marked the end of the line for Jerome Bettis, who announced his retirement while clutching the silver Vince Lombardi Trophy in his hands. He completed a journey of 13 NFL seasons in his hometown, in front of family, friends, and adoring fans.

"My teammates put me on their backs and wouldn't let me down," said Bettis, a large reason why the city of Detroit adopted the Steelers this week as their own. "I played this game to win a championship. I'm a champion. The last stop was here in Detroit

"It's been an incredible ride. Mission accomplished. With that, I have to bid farewell," Bettis said. "I'm the happiest person in the world right now.... It's better than I ever thought it would be."

Steelers Ben Roethlisberger shares a moment with head coach Bill Cowher in the closing seconds of Super Bowl XL. (Lake Fong/*Post-Gazette*)

Confetti fell like flurries from the rafters of Ford Field as NFL commissioner Paul Tagliabue presented the championship trophy—a silver football to go with the other four in the Steelers offices—to Dan Rooney and his family.

The storyline was all about The Bus, but the real motoring in Motown was by a Parker. That's Willie Parker, whose 75-yard touchdown run 22 seconds into the third quarter put the Steelers in the lead for keeps. It was the longest running play in Super Bowl history.

The score that clinched it was a bit of trickery to Hines Ward, who caught a 43-yard touchdown pass from wide receiver Antwaan Randle El, an ex-quarterback, after he took a handoff from Parker. Ward, named the game's Most Valuable Player, had 123 receiving yards on five catches and ran once for 18 yards.

"I am at a loss for words," Ward said. "There have been a lot of great MVPs who won the Super Bowl. I am speechless right now. This is truly a dream come true."

Dan Rooney, accompanied by his son Art Rooney II, accepted the prize on a special stage wheeled onto the artificial surface of Ford Field, an indoor stadium with an ear-splitting noise level.

"It's wonderful. It belongs to those right out here," Rooney said. "We're so thrilled to bring that back to Pittsburgh."

This was the 40th edition of the Super Bowl, an event now seen by a billion people around the world, but it had special meaning to a new generation of Steelers fans who had never experienced a football championship.

The changing of the guard occurred on a night that Baby Boomer favorites dominated the entertainment. After Motown's Stevie Wonder provided the pregame music and Aretha Franklin teamed with Aaron Neville to sing the national anthem, the Rolling Stones provided the signature moment. Keith Richards strummed the famous guitar riff to "Satisfaction" as Mick Jagger gyrated around the stage.

Franco Harris, MVP of the Steelers' first Super Bowl win and holder of four rings, whipped the crowd of 68,206 into a frenzy by waving a Terrible Towel during the introductions of Super Bowl greats.

The game didn't have the kind of start the Steelers wanted, and there were several anxious moments. The Seahawks had the better of the play in the first quarter and led 3–0 on a 49-yard field goal by Josh Brown.

Hines Ward (86) and Jerome Bettis celebrate alongside owner Dan Rooney after beating Seattle to win the Super Bowl. (Matt Freed/*Post-Gazette*)

The Steelers finally clicked on their fifth possession. A 21-yard shovel pass from Ben Roethlisberger to Ward got the drive started. Then facing third down with 28 yards to go, Roethlisberger connected with Ward again on a 37-yard pass that put the Steelers three yards from the goal line. Roethlisberger dove for the final yard, and referee Bill Levy upheld the call after reviewing the play.

The touchdown came with 1 minute, 55 seconds remaining in the half, and the Steelers never trailed after that.

"We played a terrible half. We knew it was a matter of time for us to get going," Bettis said.

The big electricity came on Parker's touchdown to open the second half. The Steelers had a total of 113 yards to that point, and Parker boosted that total by 75 more yards with a sprint.

"Once Willie gets through a hole, there's no way anyone is going to catch him. He's too fast," Roethlisberger said. "He broke loose and there was no one even close to him."

On their next possession, the Steelers were on the doorstep, seemingly assured of at least a field goal when Roethlisberger threw his second interception of the game. Kelly Herndon stepped in front of a pass intended for Cedrick Wilson and returned it 77 yards. Three plays later, the Seahawks made it 14–10 on a 16-yard pass from Hasselbeck to Jerramy Stevens.

But Ward's touchdown catch—on a play called "X Reverse" that Roethlisberger said was the "perfect call at the perfect time"—put the game out of reach and brought the trophy back to Pittsburgh.

"It was a big touchdown for us," Ward said. "It really sealed the thing for us."

Seattle's last offensive play was a pass that clanked off the hands of tight end Jerramy Stevens, who had engaged in a war of words with linebacker Joey Porter during the week. Stevens did catch a touchdown pass, but had several drops.

"It leaves you speechless," said linebacker Clark Haggans. "Everybody's face says it all. You can see the sweat with tears of joy coming out. It's the best feeling in all the world."

Roethlisberger, the youngest quarterback to win a Super Bowl, knelt down to kill the final three seconds.

"We got the win, and that's all that matters. Boy, it feels so good," Roethlisberger said.

In the dying seconds, Cowher took the obligatory Gatorade bath on the sideline. He raised both arms to the roof with clenched fists, then hugged his wife and daughters. Known for his fierce demeanor on the sideline, Cowher was reduced to wiping tears from his eyes after the Super Bowl win.

After Rooney handed the trophy to Cowher, the coach handed it back.

"I've been waiting a long time to do this. This is yours," Cowher said.

Later, in the locker room, Cowher tried to let it all sink in.

"It's surreal right now," Cowher said. "It is a rewarding feeling to give that trophy to Mr. Rooney. That's what he brought me here to do. It really does complete a void that's been there. I couldn't be happier for him and the city of Pittsburgh."

It was one for the ages.

Pitt Women's Basketball Team Reaches the Sweet 16

2008

Pitt's first women's basketball team took the floor for the 1914–1915 season. The program came to an end after the 1925–1926 season and wouldn't be restored until 1970. After some modest success in the 1970s, the Panthers played in four Women's National Invitational Tournaments in the 1980s and won their first Big East title in 1984. Pitt finally made it to the NCAA tournament in 2007 under coach Agnus Berenato, but lost in the second round. The following year, sparked by junior All-American Shavonte Zellous, Pitt advanced to the Sweet 16 after defeating Wyoming and Baylor. In 2009 Pitt repeated its NCAA performance the year before and advanced again to the Sweet 16. Zellous finished her career as the third leading scorer in Pitt's women basketball history and was selected in the first round of the 2009 WNBA draft by the Detroit Storm. She made the WNBA All-Rookie team in her first year as a professional.

IT'S SWEET 16 FOR PITT WOMEN

Victory Cements Coach's Drive to Elite Status

March 25, 2008
By Paul Zeise
Pittsburgh Post-Gazette

Five years ago, Pitt women's basketball coach Agnus Berenato went into the West Philadelphia house of a highly recruited center from University City High School named Marcedes Walker and sold her on a dream.

That dream was simple: If Ms. Walker came to the University of Pittsburgh—a program that hadn't had a winning season in five years and had never been to the NCAA tournament—instead of one of the high-profile programs like Rutgers that was recruiting her, Ms. Berenato would make her a star and together they'd turn the Panthers into one of the best women's programs in the country.

Ms. Berenato sold two other players that year—Mallorie Winn and Karlyle Lim—on the same dream and began to build a program. By year three, she had the Panthers in the WNIT; in year four, she had them in the NCAA tournament for the first time.

And that dream came one step closer to reality last night when the Panthers upset Baylor, 67–59, to advance to the Sweet 16 for the first time in school history. It is the kind of victory that Ms. Berenato called a "program-changer" and one that left no doubt that the Panthers have arrived as a major player.

"One of our basketball alumni, Debbie Lewis, came up to me after the game and gave me a big hug and told me 'I've been waiting for this for 25 years,'" Ms. Berenato said. "These kids on this team aren't that old to remember, and I want them to enjoy this right now.

"We are just delighted, we showed tremendous heart and soul, the heart of a lion and I'm just really proud of these girls and especially our seniors, Mallorie Winn, Marcedes Walker, and Karlyle Lim, for all of the sacrifices they've made and all of the struggles they've been through to make this moment possible.

"What those three have done for this program, they've changed it forever."

Ms. Lewis, who is a dentist and the head girls' basketball coach at Pittsburgh

Schenley High School, didn't decide to make the trip to Albuquerque until last Wednesday but felt there was something special about this team and felt they'd do something special this past weekend. It took everything in her power not to shed a few tears, and by the end of the game, she wore an ear-to-ear smile, one that she said won't go away any time soon.

"This was it, for all of us who have been around this program since the beginning, this is something special," Ms. Lewis said. "For years and years, we've taken a back seat to programs like Penn State and watched local kids go elsewhere—but it doesn't get any bigger than this, the Sweet 16 and it is Pitt going there. Agnus has built this program to the point where it is something that will put a spotlight on women's basketball in our area for a long time.

"When I go home, I can't wait to talk to all of the players from my era and many friends I have who played at Pitt over the years, this is something we'll talk about for ages. It doesn't matter what happens from here on in, this memory for me—watching Pitt win like this—will last forever. And young girls and players now can look at Pitt and know they don't need to go anywhere else to play big-time basketball. This was something special."

Ms. Walker, Ms. Winn, and Ms. Lim weren't the only people Ms. Berenato sold her dream to in 2003; she won over Pitt's athletic administration as well. And it didn't take long for her to take the university community by storm.

Pitt Chancellor Mark Nordenberg, in fact, has become one of the team's biggest fans, and he said a lot of it has to do with the fact that every time they take the court, they make the university proud. He said he never doubted that Ms. Berenato would get the job done; he just didn't think it would happen this fast.

"I really don't think that any of us had any idea this program would be built this fast," Mr. Nordenberg said last night via telephone. "This was a great night for Pitt, but on a grander scale it was also a great night for women's sports in Pittsburgh. And it is more than just the fact that this team has good basketball players—these are good students, they are role models, and they play with a lot of passion. They will be celebrated and deservedly so.

"I think that I have learned a lot and we all can learn a lot from watching Agnus build this program over the past five years."

Although the victory was a big one from an historical perspective—consider, last year was the first year the Panthers had ever been to the NCAA tournament—it got an added boost from the fact that the Panthers knocked off a perennial powerhouse in women's basketball—Baylor.

Just three years ago the Lady Bears won the national championship, they had been to the Sweet 16 three out of the last four years and they are coached by one of the profession's biggest stars—Kim Mulkey. By beating them, the Panthers proved they can compete with the elite programs and in many ways validated that this two-year run is more than just a fluke.

Pitt athletic director Steve Pederson said that he expects many more nights like last night because he's been around a lot of big-time programs and clearly Ms. Berenato has built the Panthers, who have won 20 or more games for three years in a row—another first—into one.

"Agnus has never been afraid to say she's going to win a national championship some day, and that's the kind of coach I want at every program here at Pitt," Mr. Pederson said. "She's never backed down from that but she has built this program, slowly, steadily and made into a program—not just a good team, a program that is built for the long haul.

"There were probably a lot of people who told her not to take this job when she did because of the shape that it was in, but she's been a believer and she's inspired us all and proven that you can reach incredible heights if you get good people and you have a good plan."

48

Steelers Win a Sixth Super Bowl against the Arizona Cardinals

2009

Three years after winning their fifth Lombardi Trophy and tying the Cowboys and the 49ers for the most Super Bowl championships, the Steelers were back in the Super Bowl. To become the most successful franchise in Super Bowl history, they had to defeat quarterback Kurt Warner and the Arizona Cardinals' high-flying offense. Under second year coach Mike Tomlin, the Steelers, after winning their division, had defeated the Chargers and the Ravens in the AFC playoffs. The Steelers-Cardinals Super Bowl proved to be one of the most exciting and dramatic in the event's history. The Steelers, sparked by James Harrison's 100-yard interception return for a touchdown on the last play of the first half, took a lead into the second half, but fell behind late in the fourth quarter. Ben Roethlisberger led the Steelers back and threw a six-yard touchdown pass on a spectacular catch by Santonio Holmes with 35 seconds left in the game to win the Super Bowl. Holmes became the third Steelers wide receiver to be named Super Bowl MVP.

LORDS OF THE RINGS

Harrison's Immaculate Interception, Holmes' Dramatic Reception Seal the Steelers Sixth Super Bowl Victory, 27–23

February 2, 2009
By Robert Dvorchak
Pittsburgh Post-Gazette

TAMPA, FLORIDA—It's one for the other thumb.

Santonio Holmes made an acrobatic touchdown catch with 35 seconds remaining in a heart-stopping comeback, allowing the Steelers to become the first team to win six Super Bowls. It earned Holmes a ring and the trophy as the game's MVP.

"It's going down in history," Holmes said after his catch gave the Steelers a dramatic 27–23 victory over the Arizona Cardinals in Super Bowl XLIII. "All I did was extend my arms and use my toes."

The Steelers, with the league's No. 1 defense, had blown a 13-point fourth-quarter lead as Larry Fitzgerald caught two touchdown passes, giving him a record seven touchdown catches in the postseason.

That lead was built on James Harrison's 100-yard interception return for a touchdown on the last play of the first half, which became the longest play in Super Bowl history.

If north, east, south, west, up, and down are known as the six cardinal directions, add a new twist that sends Holmes to Disney World and brings the Lombardi Trophy back home to form a sextet.

"The Super Bowl is a test, at one point, of who wants the game more than the other guy," Harrison said.

Harrison, who capped a magic year after being named team MVP and the league's defensive player of the year. "All 11 guys on the field helped out on that play."

Harrison's 100-yard return of a Kurt Warner pass showed how much he wanted it. Out of gas after an exhausting run, the linebacker just made it to the end zone as two Cardinals finally brought him to the ground. The score held up after a replay challenge.

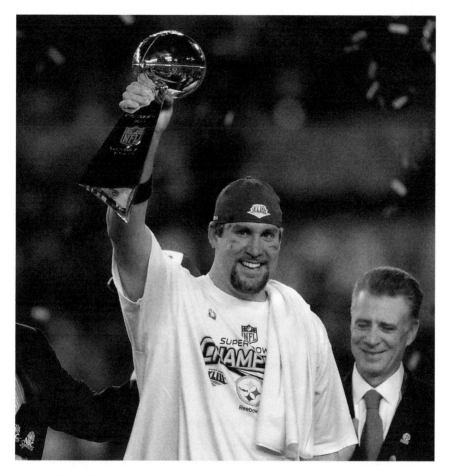

Steelers QB Ben Roethlisberger raises the Vince Lombardi Trophy and team president Art Rooney II applauds after the Steelers won their sixth Super Bowl. (Matt Freed/*Post-Gazette*)

A championship is the Pittsburgh version of seventh heaven, and there's no limit on how many will be satisfactory.

"It never gets old, that's for sure. We'll take as many as we can get," said team president Art Rooney II.

The Lombardi Trophy was presented to his father, Dan, by Hall of Famer Joe Namath.

In accepting the trophy, chairman Dan Rooney thanked President Barack Obama, who made his first congratulatory phone call as commander-in-chief to a man who supported him in the election.

Asked if there was room in the trophy case for a sixth one, Mr. Rooney answered: "We'll make room."

The Steelers passed Dallas and San Francisco, who had won five Super Bowls. The Green Bay Packers have won 12 NFL titles, nine of which were won before the Super Bowl came into existence. Still, the Steelers can claim six degrees of separation over the rest of the pack.

It was a fitting season-ending game for Harrison.

"He epitomizes what the Steelers organization is all about," fellow linebacker James Farrior said. "He's a tough, hard-nosed guy. He plays with a chip on his shoulder. He always plays aggressive, and I definitely think he's the most intimidating player out there. He doesn't have to talk. He just goes out there and plays."

It was the Steelers' second Lombardi Trophy in four years, and the sixth in 34 years. Ben Roethlisberger, who engineered the final drive with the clock ticking away, became the 10th quarterback to win at least two Super Bowls.

"We won it for the fans. I know they're going crazy back in Pittsburgh," Mr. Roethlisberger said. "It's special to win one for the Rooneys."

The Super Bowl is supposed to be a neutral site, but once again, legions of Steelers fans took over Raymond James Stadium so overwhelmingly it looked like Heinz Field South.

Throughout the week, black and gold stood out among the palm trees and azure waters of Tampa Bay. It was said more than once and in more than one establishment by the local citizenry—they had never seen fans provide such passionate support or say how proud they were to be from Pittsburgh.

The swirl and swagger remained with the Terrible Towel, which was desecrated last week by Phoenix mayor Phil Gordon. He stomped on one after using it to blow his nose at a Cardinals rally.

As heart-pounding as the game was, sixes seemed to be the order of the night. During the halftime show, Bruce Springsteen rocked on his six-string guitar while singing "Glory Days."

During the week in Tampa, the Rooneys were asked repeatedly to explain the Steeler success. They most often pointed to the stability at the head coaching positions, but coaches and players say it begins with ownership.

"We are under the leadership of Dan and Art Rooney. Their vision of what Steeler football is all about is very clear," said Mike Tomlin, who at 36 became the youngest coach to win a Super Bowl.

Steelers WR Santonio Holmes celebrates the winning touchdown in Super Bowl XLIII. (Peter Diana/*Post-Gazette*)

In summarizing the game, the coach said: "Steeler football is 60 minutes. It's never going to be pretty. Throw style points out the window, but these guys will fight to the end. We didn't blink."

In the end, it was a victory for the organization.

"It's a credit to the Rooneys," said safety Ryan Clark. "It's a credit to how they live their lives, how they run their organization, how they treat their team. They've done things the right way," he said.

To deep six something is to discard it, which is what the Steelers did to their lead. But the Cardinals' hopes went six feet under in the final moments, despite being the first team ever to rally from a deficit of 10 or more points.

The Cardinals have played in more cities than they've won titles in the last 61 years, and the Super Bowl loss was crushing because they thought they had it in their grasp.

The Cardinals were in Chicago in 1947 when they claimed the NFL championship and have moved to St. Louis and Phoenix in the interim. The drought is the longest in football and second in sports only to the century-long travails of the Chicago Cubs. The Steelers have actually won more Super Bowls than the Cardinals have playoff victories in their 89-year history.

"We wanted it more," said Santonio Holmes.

49

Penguins Win
Third Stanley Cup

2009

After winning two Stanley Cups in the early 1990s, the Penguins moved deeper and deeper into debt and by the end of the decade faced bankruptcy and a move to another city. For the second time in his career, Mario Lemeiux rescued the Penguins, this time by deferring his salary, finding new investors, and becoming the first player-owner in NHL history. Faced with a difficult financial period, the Penguins began to fall in the standings. Their misfortune on the ice, however, turned into good fortune in the NHL draft lottery. Beginning with the 2003 draft, their first round picks were Marc-Andre Fleury, Evgeni Malkin, and Sidney Crosby. Led by "Sid the Kid," the Penguins were soon back in the playoffs. In 2008, they made it to the Stanley Cup finals, only to lose to the Detroit Red Wings. But in 2009, after trailing 3–2 in games, they tied the series on home ice, then defeated the Red Wings 2–1 on goals by Max Talbot for their third Stanley Cup. In October 2009, when *The Sporting News* published a list of the NHL's top 50 hockey players, it ranked Crosby at No. 1 and Malkin at No. 3.

THE PENGUINS MARCH TO VICTORY

Max Talbot Scores Both Goals and Marc-Andre Fleury Stymies the Defending-Champion Red Wings to Lead Pittsburgh to Its Third Stanley Cup

June 13, 2009
By Sharon Eberson
Pittsburgh Post-Gazette

DETROIT—When it came down to one game, winner take all, the Comeback Kids proved too much—too much poise, too much determination, too much Max Talbot and Marc-Andre Fleury—for the defending-champion Detroit Red Wings.

The Penguins waltzed into hostile territory and walked away with a haul of engraved silver to bring back to Pittsburgh, capping an improbable run to the franchise's third Stanley Cup championship.

The Penguins beat the Red Wings 2–1 in Game 7 last night at Joe Louis Arena. Crosby, Malkin & Co. would not be denied by this veteran Detroit team for a second straight year.

The great debate of Penguins' youth vs. Wings' experience may go on, but the kids have the hardware on their side now.

Penguins superstar Mario Lemieux didn't get to lift the Cup until his seventh season in the NHL, and now he gets to celebrate as an owner of a team laden with youngsters.

After carrying the Cup himself and watching his boss lift it, Sidney Crosby said, "It's great, he's done so much. He's at the top and this starts at the top. Mario, [general manager] Ray Shero, all the people that add to this."

This was "as big as it gets; the best day of my life," said Talbot, who scored the Penguins' two goals and matched his teammate, Ruslan Fedotenko, in that feat. Fedotenko, who did it for Tampa Bay in his first Cup win, was in tears after the victory.

"It's emotional," Fedotenko said, going back and forth from Russian to English for the various media.

Penguins players grabbed their children from the stands to pose with the Cup and stayed on the ice long after the win, while their fans who had made

Penguins captain Sidney Crosby lifts the cup after defeating Detroit in Game 7 of the Stanley Cup final. (Matt Freed/*Post-Gazette*)

the trip to Detroit stayed as well. Hundreds strong, they shared in the victory, chanting "Let's go Pens!"

This final was an uphill climb for the Penguins after losing the first two games in Detroit before bouncing back to take the next two at home, then recovering from a 5–0 drubbing in Detroit to win Game 6 at Mellon Arena and force a dramatic finale.

Winning on the road is tough enough but almost unheard of in Game 7. The last NHL team to win a Cup on the road in a Game 7 was the Montreal Canadiens, who won in Chicago in 1971.

The Penguins had their work cut out for them in a building thick with the atmosphere of 11 Stanley Cup championships and the traditional dead octopus flung to the ice, then twirled by Big Al, the Zamboni driver. There appeared to be fewer flashes of black-and-gold amid the red-and-white clad fans, and the Red Wings had a big-name booster in the house: Muhammad Ali, who stood in his Wings jersey for an ovation during a break in the action.

If the Penguins were supposed to be intimidated, someone forgot to tell them.

Talbot, in particular, took no notice. At the end of two periods it was Talbot 2, Red Wings 0. The other drama was whether Crosby would return after he took a huge hit and limped into the locker room. The cameras caught Crosby's mom, Trina, hands clasped, watching, until Crosby finally emerged from the runway for the third period. Crosby stepped out for a faceoff midway through the period, but left after 32 seconds.

Talbot had scored at 1:14 of the second, before the fans had settled back from the break between periods.

Evgeni Malkin's assist on the Talbot goal gave him 36 points in these playoffs—only Lemieux and Wayne Gretzky have scored more in a single season.

The collective gasp heard around Pittsburgh came when a hard hit by Johan Franzen lifted Crosby along the boards and pinned the captain's knee, sending him limping to the locker room. A few seconds later, at 6:16, Hal Gill was banished for holding, but the Penguins weathered the storm.

With Crosby still missing in action, it was Talbot again, taking advantage of a 2-on-1 break set up by Chris Kunitz and Rob Scuderi, who gave the Pens a 2–0 lead that they took into the third period.

The Red Wings finally solved Fleury with a wobbly shot by Jonathan Ericsson with just under five minutes to play, and the crowd was back in it. The Wings dinged one shot off the post with 2½ minutes to play, and Fleury made two huge saves to clinch it.

The bearded Penguins mobbed each other on the ice as the stunned Red Wings stood or sat where they were and wondered how this one had slipped away.

The win was particularly sweet for Fleury, who took a lot of heat after the Pens were down two games to none in the finals.

Last night, the goalie was steady behind a solid defense and he even got a

Marc-Andre Fleury makes a first-period save against Detroit. (Matt Freed/*Post-Gazette*)

lucky bounce in Joe Louis Arena—imagine that—when a puck got past him but hit the crossbar and sailed out of harm's way.

The Pens' big guns were blazing during the regular season and in the play-offs. Hart Trophy finalist and postseason point leader Malkin, 22, had a career year, leading the league with 113 points and taking the Conn Smythe Trophy as the playoff MVP. Crosby, 21, the first pick overall in the 2005 draft, was third in scoring during the regular season and goal leader throughout the playoffs with 15.

Crosby was the youngest team captain to ever hoist the Cup in victory and give it a big smooch.

After the Penguins' kids pressed the Red Wings in the Stanley Cup final last year, Pittsburgh got off to a shaky start this season.

With their record at 27–25–5 on February 15, a major shake-up was deemed necessary and Dan Bylsma took over as coach, ascending from the minor-league team in Wilkes-Barre to replace Michel Therrien. Among the notable results was the improvement of the penalty-killing unit, which ranked 20th when Bylsma arrived and went on to finish eighth in efficiency.

With the pieces falling into place during the regular season, the Penguins went on 10-1-2 roll in March and Bylsma ended up the first coach to begin a season coaching an American Hockey League team and finish it behind the bench of a Stanley Cup finalist.

Bylsma said pushing his team to "play at a pace that makes it tough for other teams to play with us" relates back to his early days with the Penguins. "I think the biggest thing about what happened since February is how quickly the guys said that's the way we need to play," he said.

"Where we've come since last year at this time, since the start of the season, since February 15, wherever you want to pick up the story line from, it's an amazing thing to have accomplished and earned."

It was the stretch leading up to the playoffs that Crosby was referring to before the hard-fought Game 6 win in Pittsburgh, when the Penguins had faced elimination. He proved prophetic:

"I think we're going to bounce back. We have all year."

General Manager Shero, who had acquired the now-reviled Red Wing Marian Hossa for the Pens' stretch run a season ago, did his part again this season, bringing in new linemates for Crosby, Kunitz and Bill Guerin. With Craig Adams, Shero had added three players whose names were already on the Stanley Cup (Kunitz with Anaheim, Guerin with Dallas, Adams with Carolina).

The Detroit franchise and five of its players on ice last night had been trying for their fifth Cup victory in recent years.

The Penguins won the Cup for the first time since back-to-back championships in 1990–91 and '91–92.

50

Pittsburgh Named
Top Sports City

2009

In the same October 2009 issue that had a list of the top 50 NHL hockey players, *The Sporting News* published its annual list of the best sports cities. Out of the 399 cities listed, Pittsburgh was named No. 1, supplanting Boston from the previous year. Pittsburgh has been a great sports city since the days of Honus Wagner, Pop Warner, and Harry Greb. In the 1970s, it became the city of champions when its sports teams completely dominated the decade. In 1979 both the Pirates and the Steelers won championships, while two of the city's sports heroes, Terry Bradshaw and Willie Stargell were MVPs of their leagues. In 2009, after the Steelers won their record-breaking sixth Super Bowl and the Penguins their third Stanley Cup, Pittsburgh was once again the city of champions and, even with the Pirates setting a record for consecutive losing seasons, was now nationally recognized and acclaimed as the best sports city in America.

PITTSBURGH CHALKS UP ANOTHER SPORTS WIN

City Named No. 1 By *The Sporting News*

October 8, 2009
By Timothy McNulty
Pittsburgh Post-Gazette

It took 16 years, but on-a-roll Pittsburgh has finally been named the No. 1 sports city by *The Sporting News*, beating out 398 other towns in the United States and Canada.

The city was so anointed largely on the backs of the dual 2009 Steelers and Penguins championships, but don't tell that to the former Luke Steelerstahl.

"I don't know how we don't win this every year," mayor Luke Ravenstahl said at the announcement, held in his City-County Building conference room with *The Sporting News* publisher Ed Baker.

The magazine's cover pairs Sidney Crosby and Ben Roethlisberger, and the 29-year-old mayor noted its resemblance to an iconic *Sports Illustrated* cover with Willie Stargell and Terry Bradshaw from 1979. Times are a little bit better now, and *The Sporting News* designation gave Mr. Ravenstahl a chance to crow again about good publicity for the city. Keep in mind Mr. Ravenstahl is a sports nut who ceremoniously changed his name in January, walked a Super Bowl red carpet in Tampa, and is in a charity fantasy football league with other mayors this fall.

"We are in many ways in the national and international spotlight right now because of the G-20 and the economic revitalization of this town.... It's a great day for Pittsburgh and a great day for sports fans," Mr. Ravenstahl said.

Philadelphia was second in the magazine's ratings and Boston third. Last year Boston won the honor and in 2007, Detroit.

Mr. Baker said the selection incorporates the number of teams in each city (which hurts Pittsburgh, due to the lack of pro basketball), team won-lost records (where the Pirates hurt the ranking), and a lot of things that go in the city's favor, such as playoff records, attendance, and fan ferocity.

"There's some science, some math, and some subjectivity attached to it," Mr. Baker said.

The issue hits newsstands this week. It contains an eight-page spread on Pittsburgh sports, with stories on Western Pennsylvania quarterbacks, Pitt versus West Virginia, Steelers Super Bowl rings, and tips from ex-Pirates on making the team a winner again.

"I think it's a great time to reflect on how lucky we are as Pittsburghers and how lucky we are to have the great fans we have, not only in the city of Pittsburgh but around the world. I hope our fans realize this is a great tribute to them as well," Steelers spokesman Dave Lockett said.

Penguins spokesman Tom McMillan—wearing a giant Stanley Cup championship ring on his right hand—noted that Penguins, Steelers, and Pirates players routinely attend each other's games. "That is really unique. That doesn't happen in most cities," he said.

Pittsburgh has piled up similar awards to *The Sporting News* one lately— *Forbes* said the Penguins were the fastest-growing brand in hockey this year, and last year's Turnkey Team Brand Index rated the Steelers third in overall brand loyalty after the Packers and Red Sox.

Mr. Baker, the magazine publisher, gave the mayor a Tiffany vase to mark the honor. Mr. Ravenstahl's ornate office already has a number of sports items in it, including a framed football jersey and Tiffany football given to late Mayor Bob O'Connor to mark the Steelers Super Bowl win in 2006.

The mayor—who after the news conference talked to reporters about the city's perspective on the cash-strapped Carnegie Library system—talked about the escape Pittsburgh's sports fandom supplies.

"People find comfort and unity in sports and it's an escape for them.... On a Monday morning, you don't have to pick up the newspaper to know if the Steelers won or not. You just have to walk around town and get the sense of people.... That really speaks volumes to the intensity of fans here and how much we interact with the teams," he said.

AFTERWORD

New Town Team vs. Old Towne Team

May 28, 2003
By David M. Shribman
Pittsburgh Post-Gazette

This space is reserved for essays on the moral conundrums of our time, the difficult questions of enduring social importance, the epochal matters involving eternal themes. Great issues like Loyalty. Responsibility. Justice. Redemption. The Red Sox.

Nearly four months ago, I moved to a great new town and got a great new start. It was exhilarating in every way: new surroundings, new challenges, new opportunities, new friends, a new league (the National League), a new stadium (PNC Park is baseball's prettiest), and a new team—the Pirates.

Now the Boston Red Sox are coming to town to ruin everything.

For four decades these same Sox have toyed with me, disappointed me, hurt me. They have broken my heart and have almost broken my spirit. They haven't won the World Series in my lifetime. Nor in my father's. Strom Thurmond, not known to be a Red Sox man, was, however, alive the last time the World Series flag flew over Fenway.

This is all you need to know about these bums: They have finished second to the Yankees for five consecutive seasons. Yes, they have taught me the value of patience. (It has been 85 years since they've won the championship, so those of us in Red Sox Nation know not to wait till next year. We wait till next century.) But they have also taught me about the vanity of human wishes. (I'm more likely to be hit by a meteorite than to witness a World Series celebration in Kenmore Square.) Some people have demons. I have Johnny Damon.

So the moral question I face at the interleague games next week is clear: Do I root for my new team in my new town? Or do I stick with the Olde Towne Team, as the Sox are sometimes called?

For most of my colleagues in the columnizing business, this is a trivial digression, eclipsed in significance by the budget deficit (going up), the tax burden (going down), civic participation (going away), and the reconstitution of Iraq (going badly). But I am tormented by whether to support the team led by Grady Little (the Sox manager, still going strong) or Lloyd McClendon (the Bucs' manager, who may be going, going, gone).

Wouldn't it be disloyal to my New England roots to abandon the Red Sox, whom I first visited in their cozy ballpark in 1962 (it was a no-hitter)? But wouldn't it also be disloyal to my new colleagues and neighbors to abandon the Pirates, whose fortunes I have eagerly embraced since coming to the *Post-Gazette* (some nights they have no hitters)? Put another way: Is it noble to refuse to change? Or is it ennobling to have the courage to change?

I am tortured by this question—though my publisher, my wife, and my daughters all believe I have more important things to worry about, or ought to. Then again, I did invite Yaz, whom I had never met, to our wedding. (Carl Yastrzemski, my boyhood hero, didn't show. Cindy Skrzycki, my fiancee, did. Two great Polish Americans, one great lesson.)

On the surface, there is no reason to dread next week's three-game series. It's the first time the two teams have met in an entire century—since the 1903 World Series, the very first. Cy Young pitched in four games. Honus Wagner came to the plate 30 times. Pittsburgh that year was the richest city on earth, its people open-minded and fiercely optimistic. Boston was static and stubbornly staid, possessed of a Puritan pessimism that it didn't shake until the late 1960s. My two towns have nothing in common, except everything.

"The story of the first World Series is the story of the birth of baseball as a modern game," writes Louis P. Masur, a professor of history at City College of New York who, presumably, also has more important things to worry about, or ought to. His *Autumn Glory: Baseball's First World Series* is one of three books on the 1903 World Series to be published this season. Somewhere in this favored land is someone who has read all three.

I sat in the back row of the bleachers when the Red Sox, hundred-to-one odds to win the 1967 American League pennant, clinched the title when Rico Petrocelli caught an infield pop-up for the last out on the last pitch of the last day of the season. I saw Yaz slam two homers and Jim Lonborg throw a one-hitter in the second game of the Series that October, against the St. Louis Cardinals. I spent a lot of the *Wall Street Journal's* money to fly to a Senate debate in Idaho only to sneak out and rush into a bar in Coeur d'Alene and stare, incredulously, at a ceiling-mounted television as Bill Buckner muffed a routine ground ball in the sixth game of the 1986 Series. The most memorable day I ever spent with my older daughter—we agree on this—was in Fenway when we saw Pedro Martinez beat Roger Clemens in an American League Championship Series game. We framed the tickets, one for her room, one for my office. Boston and the Red Sox are my past.

But I was stirred in early April by the way the lights went out at PNC Park on Opening Night and the fireworks filled the sky. I can't take my eyes off the Pittsburgh skyline as I watch our bumbling Bucs play in the cool evenings of a southwestern Pennsylvania spring. I even believe that if, between innings, I look long enough at that screen with the funny blue shapes mounted on the old Horne's building, I will figure out what the heck it is supposed to mean. Pittsburgh and the Pirates are my future.

Deep inside my very favorite book, *The Red Sox Reader*, is a little piece by David Halberstam, who also presumably has more important things to worry about, or ought to. This essay is about having what he calls "a soul divided." He's a New Yorker and a New Englander, a Yankees fan and a Sox partisan, which is a little like being a Republican and Roosevelt supporter in the 1938 midterm elections. No matter. He pulls it off somehow. I'm going to have to do the same. In December 1962, John F. Kennedy, a onetime Navy lieutenant, nonetheless watched the Army-Navy game from the Navy side of the field for the first half, from the Army side for the second half.

So I'll be at the ballyard next week, in Section 124. I can't bring myself to root against the Sox. I can't bring myself to root against the Pirates, either. I'll cheer, to be sure. But I'll cheer for the glory of our American game, and for the happy fact that I can see both my teams at once, on one splendid field. Mine is a tale of two cities, and next week is the best of times.

AFTERWORD

Growing Up with Clemente

April 17, 2005
By Richard "Pete" Peterson

When 20-year-old outfielder Roberto Clemente made his major-league debut with the Pittsburgh Pirates on Sunday, April 17, 1955, I was a 16-year-old outfielder with the South High Orioles varsity baseball team.

Like most Pittsburgh kids in the late 1940s, my early baseball hero had been home-run king Ralph Kiner, but when I became a Little League pitcher in 1951, my hero-worshipping became more practical. I was short and skinny and didn't throw that hard, so the Pirates' crafty, rubber-armed pitcher Murry Dickson became my idol. By the time I went out for my high school baseball team in 1955, I was playing the outfield and needed another new hero. The challenge was finding a decent outfielder on a Pirates team that had finished in last place for the past three years.

It should have been a match made in baseball heaven. The reports coming out of Pirates spring training claimed that Clemente was a natural, and I badly needed a Pirates outfielder who could actually run, field, and throw. The only problem was Clemente himself. I was living on the South Side, at that time a shot-and-a-beer neighborhood defined by its ethnic enclaves, its steel-mill mentality, and its deep distrust of minorities. My working-class father and his beer-joint buddies, while diehard Pirates fans, believed that black ballplayers were ruining baseball, and I was my father's son. I had plenty of help in my early prejudice against black ballplayers.

Despite the presence of Branch Rickey in the front office since 1951, the Pirates, with their white working-class fan base, had been very slow to sign minorities. Among Clemente's teammates at the beginning of the 1955 season was second-baseman Curt Roberts who, in 1954, seven years after Jackie Robinson crossed baseball's color line and the same year of the Brown v. Board of Education decision, became the first African American to play in a Pirates uniform. Roberts had been an outstanding minor-league ballplayer, but he pushed himself too hard and slumped badly in 1954. He was still in the starting line-up when the Pirates opened the 1955 season in Brooklyn, but he didn't start at second base when Clemente made his major-league debut three days later. After appearing in only six games in 1955, Roberts was sent back to the minor leagues.

I was also getting reinforcement for my "Souseside" prejudice from the sports sections of Pittsburgh's three daily newspapers. I was familiar with Clemente's Puerto Rican heritage because sportswriters exaggerated and made fun of his accent in their stories and columns: "One theeng I like Merica, new autos. Buy myself new auto. Whee!" is but one example. Exploiting Clemente's flamboyant play, they also portrayed him as a Puerto Rican hot dog and mocked his injuries by describing him as a whining hypochondriac.

This stereotype of Clemente lasted beyond his rookie season. In 1960, despite his outstanding season in leading the Pirates to the National League pennant, scouting reports on the World Series that were appearing in national magazines denigrated Clemente. Writing for *Life* magazine, Jim Brosnan, who had won critical praise for his bestselling *The Long Season*, described Clemente's play as "a Latin-American variety of showboating; 'Look at Numero Uno,' he seems to be saying."

When Bill Mazeroski hit his dramatic home run, I was watching the game in the furniture department of the Gimbels department store Downtown, where I was an unhappily employed stockboy. By the time I made it down the escalator and onto Smithfield Street, the city had already erupted into a Mardi Gras frenzy. Clemente didn't participate in the celebration, but he believed that he had finally won the acceptance and respect of teammates, sportswriters, and fans. When the balloting for the National League Most Valuable Player Award was announced, he discovered that the honor went to Dick Groat and he had finished a distant eighth.

Convinced that his race and heritage had determined the vote, Clemente went on to play baseball in the 1960s as if it were a form of punishment for those who slighted him. He also began to speak out against racial prejudice. Clemente believed that Latin-American ballplayers were a minority within a minority, treated in the 1960s the way African-American ballplayers had been treated in the 1950s. He stated publicly that Latin Americans were commonly and unfairly dismissed by the press and some of their teammates as too temperamental, lazy and even gutless in clutch situations.

Roberto Clemente receives a standing ovation from Pirates fans after his 1971 Game 7 home run. (Edwin Morgan/*Post-Gazette*)

—

I'd like to remember that my own awareness of Clemente's humanity began in the turbulent 1960s, but I never connected the country's racial and political changes with my life as a baseball fan. I was a graduate student at Kent State when Martin Luther King Jr. was assassinated in April 1968, but I barely noticed Clemente's pivotal role in the decision by the Pirates—who had 11 black players, more than any team in the major leagues at that time—to delay their season opener, scheduled for the day of King's funeral.

I didn't really begin to appreciate Clemente's true greatness, his courage, and his pride until his flawless play in the 1971 World Series and his tragic death a little more than a year later, helping the victims of a terrible earthquake in Nicaragua.

Growing up with Clemente, I had no understanding of what he was going through because I shared the racial attitudes and feelings that made his early career so difficult. Fifty years later, I feel a sense of loss for the Clemente cut down in his greatness, but I finally also see an image of Clemente in 1955, proud of his abilities as a ballplayer and his Latin American heritage, yet emotionally alienated from America's national game because of that heritage.

No wonder on the proudest day of his baseball career, at the very moment when the baseball world was honoring his greatness in the 1971 World Series, he remembered his love of baseball and his family as the source of his emotional strength and asked his parents, and not the press or his fans, for their blessing.

ABOUT THE AUTHORS

David M. Shribman is executive editor of the *Pittsburgh Post-Gazette*. As Washington bureau chief of *The Boston Globe*, he was awarded the 1995 Pulitzer Prize for his coverage of American political culture. He has served as national political correspondent for *The Wall Street Journal*, congressional and political reporter for the *New York Times*, and feature writer for *The Washington Star*. He holds an A.B. degree, summa cum laude, from Dartmouth College, was elected to Phi Beta Kappa, and won a graduate fellowship in history at Cambridge University. He is the author of three books on Dartmouth sports and has attended more than 30 Pirates games annually for a decade.

Richard "Pete" Peterson is a Pittsburgh native and a retired English professor at Southern Illinois University. He is the editor of *The Pirates Reader* and *The St. Louis Baseball Reader* and the author of *Growing Up With Clemente* and *Extra Innings: Writing on Baseball*. His baseball essays have appeared in the *Chicago Tribune*, the *St. Louis Post-Dispatch*, and his hometown *Pittsburgh Post-Gazette*. He is also the commentator for the Reading Baseball series on the NPR Illini Network. He saw his first Pirates game at Forbes Field in 1948 at the age of nine.